IN SEARCH OF THE MIDDLE EAST

PEOPLE AND PLACES OF THE WORLD

IN SEARCH OF THE MIDDLE EAST

PUBLISHED BY THE READER'S DIGEST ASSOCIATION LIMITED
LONDON NEW YORK MONTREAL SYDNEY CAPE TOWN

Originally published in partwork form,
Des Pays et des Hommes,
by Librairie Larousse, Paris

A Reader's Digest selection

IN SEARCH OF THE MIDDLE EAST

Translated and edited by Toucan Books Limited, London
Translated and adapted by Richard Walker

ISBN 0 276 42053 5

Printed by Printer Industria Gráfica S.A., Barcelona

Contents

COVER PICTURES

Top: *The eroded cliffs of a valley in Afghanistan.*
Bottom: *A stall holder in the market at San'a, Yemen.*

The Fertile Crescent and the Lands of the Book

Around the year AD 610 a young merchant from the Arabian trading town of Mecca had a vision in which, according to the Koran, the angel Gabriel appeared to him with the proclamation, 'You are the Messenger of God'. It was a vision that would change the history of the Middle East. By 622 the young Muhammad had spread his message of *Islam*, or submission to God, so effectively and so uncompromisingly in Mecca that he had earned himself a considerable body of enemies – as well as followers – among the town's wealthy élite.

In another key moment, from which Muslims came to date the start of the Islamic Era, he fled Mecca for Medina. This was the *Hegira* (flight), after which the spread of Muhammad's teachings knew no bounds. Muhammad used the power of the sword to defend and advance his life's work. In 625 he defeated his enemies from Mecca in the battle of Badr. He went on to survive a siege of Medina two years later, and in 630 he re-entered Mecca in triumph at the head of 10,000 followers. By the time he died two years after that, he left much of Arabia united under a common leadership and in allegiance to a dynamic new faith, which over the succeeding decades and centuries would spread right across the Middle East – as well as farther east into Central Asia and the Indian sub-continent, north into Asia Minor and parts of Europe, and west across northern Africa, even reaching into Spain.

Islam remains a prime fact of life in the Middle East. Throughout the region, from Istanbul poised where Europe meets Asia in the west to Kabul perched high among the mountains of the Hindu Kush to the east, the faith of the Prophet Muhammad has left its imprint: in the minarets of mosques poking skywards above towns and cities; in the five-times daily calls to prayer wailing from them; in distinctive attitudes towards justice, the rights of women and in other areas of life. The Middle East encompasses great contrasts of scenery, from the deserts of Arabia to the wooded slopes of Turkey's Black Sea coast, from the mountains of Afghanistan to the marshes of southern Iraq. And its peoples present an equal variety: Turks, Kurds, Armenians, Arabs, Jews, Pashtuns, Baluchis and many others. Not all of them are Muslims, but Islam is the one factor none can avoid. Turkey's reform-minded leader, Kemal Atatürk, tried to wean his country off a strictly Muslim heritage in the first half of this century, and to a large extent succeeded; even so, Islam retains a vital, and once more growing, influence on Turkish affairs. Problems between Jews and Palestinians mean that Israel can never forget the importance of Islam, while the oil wealth of Saudi Arabia and Iraq – two of the world's biggest oil producers – has only added to its prominence in the 20th century. Yemen and Afghanistan have flirted with Communism but even there Islam has proved the more enduring creed.

And yet the Middle East – lying as it does near the junction of three continents: Europe, Asia and Africa – has an important heritage that stretches back considerably further than the birth of Islam, or even the region's two other native religions: Christianity and Judaism. In ancient times the so-called Fertile Crescent – spreading from Egypt up through Palestine to Anatolia (the Asian part of modern Turkey) and then down again into the valleys of the Tigris and Euphrates rivers and Mesopotamia (roughly modern Iraq) – provided ideal conditions for some of the first civilisations. Scholars estimate that the rich soils between the Tigris and Euphrates were capable of producing crops as plentiful in the millennia before Christ as those of the prairies of modern Canada. Such abundance meant a release from the demands of subsistence living and the possibility of supporting dense populations. People were able to gather together in towns and cities, and thus the first urban civilisations were born.

The earliest of these was probably the Sumerian civilisation which developed in southern Mesopotamia some time after 3000 BC. The Sumerians not only invented urban living but the earliest-known form of writing. Using the ends of reed stalks, they would inscribe rows of tiny, stylised pictures (or pictograms) on clay tablets which were then baked hard, and in this way they kept detailed records of commercial transactions. Later this developed into a 'cuneiform' script in which wedge-like marks in the clay came to stand for particular speech sounds. The Sumerians also produced the world's oldest extant work of literature, the *Epic of Gilgamesh*, telling the story of a flood remarkably similar to the Biblical account of Noah's flood.

After the early Sumerians, Mesopotamia gave birth to further civilisations and empires. The Sumerians had a last fling in the empire of Ur which collapsed around 2000 BC, after which there was a period of some turmoil – this was probably when the Biblical Abraham set out from Mesopotamia for the land of Canaan. Then some new powers started to make themselves felt. In Anatolia to the north, the Hittites had been a growing power since well before 2000 BC; in Mesopotamia, Babylon began to establish its supremacy until it ruled an empire reaching from the Persian Gulf in the south as far north as the upper reaches of the Tigris. Its most impressive ruler in this period was Hammurabi, commemorated in the Code of Hammurabi. This was an astonishing testimony to the sophistication of the Babylonians, consisting of 280 pronouncements on criminal and civil law, including libel, the property rights of married women, embezzlement and money left in trust for children.

Around 1600 BC Babylon fell to the Hittites, inaugurating another 'dark age' for Mesopotamia. Babylon revived for a while in the 12th and 11th centuries BC, in spite of the growing power of the Assyrians to the north, but lapsed into decline again in the 10th century – when, to the west, Israel was at the height of its power under King Solomon. The Assyrians, meanwhile, seemed unstoppable, and in 689 King Sennacherib (with Nineveh as his capital) captured Babylon, razing it to the ground. The tables were turned, however, and 100 years later Babylon was once more the centre of a large empire, ruled over by Nebuchadnezzar, instigator of the Israelites' Babylonian captivity. This was the Babylon which under different dynasties and rulers would survive until the 2nd century BC as a cultural and intellectual powerhouse famous for its astronomers (who may have included the 'three wise men' of Jesus's nativity).

After that the fate of most of the Middle East became entwined with the

Greek, Roman and Persian empires until Muhammad and his followers erupted on the scene with their desert-born faith in the 7th century AD. And they too would add to the cross-currents of the region's history. After the Prophet's death, leaders of the *ummah* (community) of believers chose his father-in-law Abu Bakr as his successor – or *khalifah*, caliph. But many regarded his son-in-law Ali as the more rightful heir, a division of opinion that would eventually lead to a split between Sunni traditionalists and the Shi'ite followers of Ali. In the meantime, the Muslims proved themselves a force to be reckoned with. Under the caliphs of the Umayyad dynasty – the first was Muhammad's brother-in-law Mu'awiyah – they established an Arab empire that extended from Persia in the east to Spain in the west. Following the Umayyads came the Abbasids whose capital Baghdad became one of the most glittering cities in the world.

By the end of the 9th century, however, the unity of the Muslim world was broken. In the centuries that followed it would be torn between rival caliphs and other rulers and realms, and threatened periodically by Christian Crusaders from the west and Mongol hordes from the east. And yet, for all that, Islam went on making converts and continued to produce remarkable leaders and military successes. In the 12th century the great Kurdish hero Saladin played havoc with the Crusaders and managed to win Jerusalem back for the Muslims. By the late 14th century the Turkish Ottomans were beginning to make their presence felt. They suffered a temporary setback at the hands of the Mongol warlord Tamerlane, but recovered sufficiently to capture Constantinople in 1453. Their sultans would go on to claim the title of caliph and rule a huge empire that once more imposed a large measure of political unity on the Middle East – not to mention parts of eastern Europe. It would finally crumble, after a long period as the 'sick man of Europe', only at the beginning of this century.

In the light of such a history, it is hardly surprising that the Middle East is what it is today: a patchwork of peoples and cultures as diverse as the city-dwellers of Baghdad, the Marsh Arabs of southern Iraq, Iraq's Assyrian Christians, the newly rich Bedouins of Saudi Arabia and the highland tribespeople of Yemen. And the 20th century has also brought a series of new encounters and alignments. The First World War was followed by the emergence of new states from the ruins of the Ottoman Empire. Then came the realignment of power and influence following the discovery of oil, as well as events such as the foundation of a Jewish state after the Second World War and the rise of Islamic fundamentalism. All this has put huge strains on societies that have had to absorb new values and circumstances in a few decades – on top of which there has been the constant threat, and reality, of military strife: the Arab-Israeli wars, the Soviet invasion of Afghanistan, the Gulf War.

But perhaps what is more remarkable is the extent to which the Middle East has, by and large, succeeded in adapting to the new world. Stresses and strains there have been – but large numbers of ordinary people in the Middle East remain faithful to their traditional ways and beliefs. Despite the pressures of the modern world, the power of continuity seems to be at least as strong as that of change in a region that has produced such a dazzling succession of civilisations since the ancient Sumerians first started carrying out their transactions in writing.

Turkey

The Golden Horn and the Bosporus, a skyline dominated by domes and minarets and the serene profile of St Sophia, the ancient names of Byzantium and Constantinople – all these and more add their lustre to the romance and fascination of Istanbul. But there is more, of course, to Turkey than its most famous city. Almost all the great civilisations of the ancient world spread their rule or influence to its lands. And while its past tells a story of alternating tumult and splendour, its present reveals a unique mingling of East with West – a surprising, engaging, though sometimes explosive, mix of widely differing outlooks and traditions.

Previous page:
'The road of progress must be trodden by both sexes', instructed Atatürk, but the Turkish woman remains a victim of double standards — especially in rural areas where traditions of male dominance run deep.

Industrial grime rims the Golden Horn but cannot quite destroy its visual splendour. The once pristine waters of the legendary anchorage became a reeking sewer lined with factories, slaughterhouses and fetid slums, but many eyesores have been removed as part of a programme to restore some of its lost grandeur.

Sardine-like hamsi, *courgettes and spices sizzle in a giant frying pan by the water's edge. The streets of Istanbul are filled with inviting aromas; and one can eat well for next to nothing.*

The Land Between Two Worlds

It is almost dawn on the Greek-Turkish border. At Kastanies, a Greek cock crow rakes the receding night. From out of the dark, a faint voice seems to respond, followed by another. 'Allahu Akbar . . . God is most great . . . I testify there is no god but God . . . I testify that Muhammad is the messenger of God . . . Come to prayer . . . Prayer is better than sleep . . .'

Turkey is somewhere out there, being awakened by the call of the muezzins. Above the blackness that still cloaks the rolling fields of Thrace, the traveller senses a silhouette of intoxicating grandeur that gradually resolves itself into the dome and minarets of the Selimiye Mosque, rising above the lesser domes and red-tiled roofs of Edirne.

For maximum impact, this is how to come upon the land of the Turks: on foot, at break of day, passing from the linear simplicity of the Greek village into this place of crumbling monuments, teeming bazaars and cobbled streets. Edirne is a living museum of the heyday of the Ottoman Empire; when the sultans and their fearsome janissaries held all Europe at bay.

Edirne, or Adrianople, was once Hadrianopolis – the city of Hadrian – a fortress on a loop of the River Tunca. It was built by the same Roman emperor who walled in England, and it has been a stepping stone for conquerors ever since. Here the Goths broke through to begin the dismemberment of the Roman Empire, and subsequent uninvited guests included the Bulgars (in 814, 911, 1002, and again in 1912), the Crusaders (1101 and 1147), the Russians (1829 and 1878) and the Greeks (1920). Between times were 500 years of ease as a royal retreat of the Ottomans, which accounts for the quantity and quality of the old mosques, tombs, caravanserais, and more than 30 *hamams* (Turkish baths), some of which are 600 years old. There is even the world's first mental hospital, in which inmates were serenaded by a ten-piece orchestra and fed pheasant and partridge. Islam holds the insane to be 'touched by the hand of God', which might account for such enlightenment in the 15th century.

Edirne's travail resumed with the decline of the Ottoman Empire in the 19th century, and it changed hands eight times before coming to a rickety rest in the tiny sliver of Europe retained by modern Turkey. Crossed by speeding trucks and tourist traffic, it goes about its business in a scurrying sort of way. Every little awning or hole in the wall seems to harbour a vendor, whether of melon chunks or splendidly polished old shoes. The streets nowadays are an obstacle course of roadworks that ensnare an overload of horse-drawn carts, not to mention vintage American cars painted

The fish is guaranteed fresh, the waters perhaps less so, but regulars swear by the food served beside the steamer terminals, where the Horn flows into the Bosporus. Turks believe the setting is an important part of a meal, and that fish is best eaten near the source. Every corner of Istanbul is staked out in this way by people striving to make a living of some kind.

candy pink and seeing out their days as *dolmus* ('filled') communal taxis.

One has only to glance upwards and there is the reassuring, enduring perfection of the Selimiye Cami, so ethereal that it seems pinned down only by its four needle-slim minarets. Mosque design reached its apogee with this structure, the acknowledged masterpiece of Sinan, architect to Süleiman the Magnificent, a contemporary of Henry VIII and Elizabeth I of England.

Knowing about Mimar Sinan (Sinan the architect) is a first step towards appreciating the complexities of Turkish culture. Although his parents were Greek Orthodox Christians, he was drafted into the service of the Ottoman Empire at the age of 23, making his name initially as an artillery officer in the army. He first revealed his architectural talents with bridges and military fortifications, and only completed his first non-military building when he was 50 years old. He made up amply for this late start, however. By the time he died in 1588, a year short of his 100th birthday – he was already in his eighties when he was supervising the construction of the Selimiye Mosque – he had built 79 mosques (including the Sehzade Mosque and the Mosque of Süleiman the Magnificent in Istanbul), 34 palaces, 33 public baths, as well as numerous schools, fountains, aqueducts and hospitals. Mimar Sinan was undoubtedly the greatest and most influential architect the Ottoman Empire produced. And despite his Christian upbringing it was he who, with his genius for fusing light and space into sanctuaries of boundless tranquillity, infused Islamic architecture with a sense of the sublime.

Poor youngsters always seem to find some sort of employment – often something to sell. These little loaves are still warm from the oven.

The oil wrestlers

Modern invaders rarely have much time for such thoughts as they head from the border at full throttle, intent upon reaching Istanbul as quickly as possible. Nowadays the road of the Roman legions is the E4 motorway, better known to the locals as the *Londra Asfalta* for its most distant connection – London. So Edirne is largely left to its own devices as the market town of the Thracian plain, where the melons are the sweetest on earth and where every summer strongmen come from all over Turkey to wrestle.

Güres (wrestling) is a national obsession comparable only to soccer. Almost any kind of wrestling will do (crowds turn out to witness camels wrestle), but *yagli güres,* or oil wrestling, is the biggest crowd-puller. Hundreds of local champions arrive from all corners of Turkey for the annual five-day tournament held on an islet to the north of Edirne, all eager for glory and the opportunity to escape the rural grind that is the lot of most. They can be easily recognised as they stroll round the town carrying their leather fighting breeches, or

The shores of the Bosporus are lined with waterfront residences, including centuries-old wooden yali, *some with dozens of rooms, which are much in demand as summer homes for the rich of Istanbul.*

Porters called hamal *perform prodigious feats of strength and endurance carrying goods around the clogged and narrow streets of Istanbul. The more backbreaking the load, the greater the prestige – and the pay.*

*Teetering antique pine houses (*kösk*), each home to numerous families, cling to some of the little streets that clamber up from the Istanbul waterfront. Eventually they will fall to the bulldozer, to be replaced by more concrete flat blocks.*

'May Allah guide him of truest heart to victory!' With this invocation, and a final slick-down from the oil can, a pair of oil wrestlers set to work. Most are farm workers, often shepherds from Anatolia, and this is their one chance for fame and a little fortune to supplement their meagre income. Prizes in cash and goods are put up by local businessmen. Losers can always consider joining Turkey's big migrant labour force abroad.

Yagli güres – *oil wrestling – is popular throughout Turkey. The premier tournament at Kirkpinar, near Edirne, is said to date from 1360, which would make it the longest-running sporting event in the world.*

Oil wrestling fans are knowledgeable and demanding. Betting is brisk, and a listless match will earn their noisy scorn. Turkish culture exults the warrior almost in the manner of old Japan.

kispet, in wicker baskets. Funfairs and gypsy carnivals sprout up around the arena, with diversions ranging from bingo to dancing bears, and the aromas of roast lamb and mint tea hang heavy in the air.

The contest is preceded by prayers at the Selimiye Mosque, a bull sacrifice, and by fanfares of whining fifes and booming drums as the wrestlers take the field. They slick themselves all over with olive oil, diluted so that they do not fry in the sun. Paired off, the glistening gladiators turn towards Mecca to praise God, and the *cazgir* (master of ceremonies) delights the crowd with colourful descriptions of each man's prowess. The object is much the same as in conventional freestyle wrestling, but pinning an opponent is not easy under such slithery circumstances; a bout may last a few minutes, sometimes much longer. The fighters pair off again and again, the ground becoming slippery with oil and sweat, and the fifes and drums toot and thump until the musicians begin to flag, usually around the third day. The prizes are small, but the honour is great, and so is the amount of betting. The Prime Minister attends on the final day to crown the *bas pehlivan*, the grand champion.

The tournament dates from 1360, according to a legend that traces its origin to 40 heroes returning from a Turkish victory. The exuberant warriors paired off to wrestle. All day and all night they grappled, until only two were undefeated; the next morning they were found still locked together, both dead from their exertions. When the army next passed that way, the men's comrades were impressed to find that the site had become a lush meadow with 40 springs bubbling from the wrestlers' graves. Sure enough, the spot is known as Kirkpinar, 'Forty Springs'.

Oil wrestling itself can be traced back to the ancient Greeks, perhaps earlier. And in this it is typical of much in modern Turkey which is sometimes likened to a palimpsest – a re-used parchment – with its past for ever peeking into the present. The list alone of the country's archaeological remains gives an idea of the depth of its heritage, starting with the Late Stone Age settlement of Çatal Hüyük in southern Turkey discovered in the 1960s. It dates from 6700 BC, and is one of the world's oldest-known towns – its inhabitants lived in mud-brick houses which they entered through a hole in the roof. The village of Bogazkale high up in the mountains east of the capital Ankara, meanwhile, is the site of another ancient city: Hattusas, capital of the Hittite Empire which flourished between 1400 and 1200 BC. On the western, Aegean coast the port city of Izmir (Smyrna), modern Turkey's third-largest city, was founded by the Greeks around 1000 BC and is believed by some scholars to have been the birthplace of the poet Homer; while to the north lie the excavated ruins of Troy where the events of his epic poem the *Iliad* were fought out.

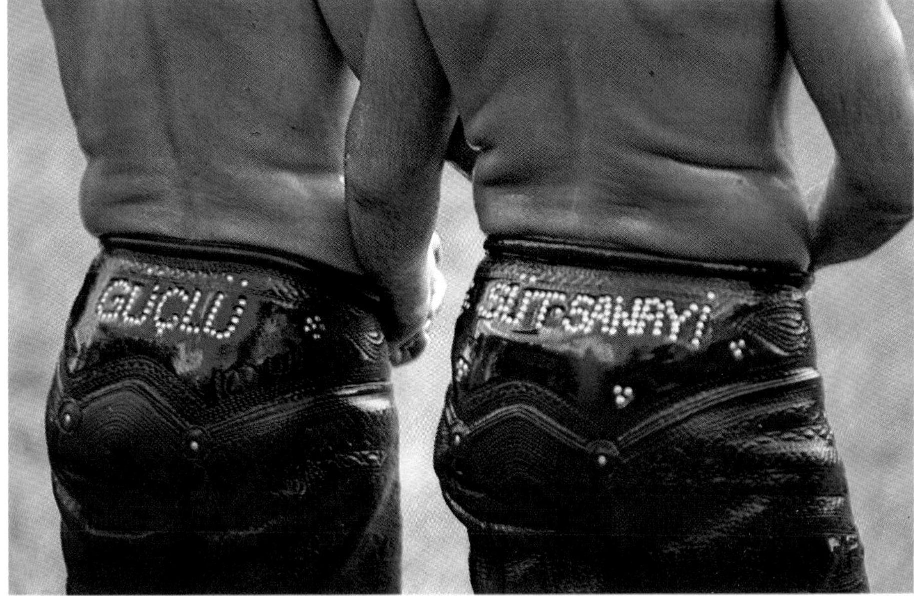

Oil wrestlers fight in sturdy made-to-measure leather breeches studded with the name of the fighter or his club. Fighters are matched according to height rather than weight.

Ephesus, farther south along the Aegean coast, had the great Temple of Artemis (or Diana), which was one of the Seven Wonders of the ancient world. The temple has vanished, but the site retains abundant sun-bleached ruins of the city that was visited by St Paul during his missionary travels – and where he ran into trouble when he lured too many of the locals away from the worship of Artemis, thus depriving many of the city's gold and silversmiths of an important part of their business. St Paul himself was born at Tarsus lying a little inland from the south coast.

Civilisations in Collision

On glossy tourist brochures Turkey likes to style itself as the 'Land of Civilisations', but 'Civilisations in Collision' might be more accurate. As the Turks themselves wryly joke, 'East is East and West is West – but Turkey is something else . . . '

Turkey is a new country in an old land, for thousands of years a cultural bridge and shifting frontier between Europe and the Middle East. Only since 1923 has it been a nation in its own right: a Western-styled secular republic carved, against all the odds, out of the heartland of a pan-Islamic empire. With a population of over 50 million people, it is the most populous country in the Middle East and a key member of NATO, guarding the alliance's south-eastern flank. It is also a member of the Council of Europe and an associate of the European Community with aspirations in the long term to become a full member of the EC.

In spite of such credentials, however, its position in

relation to Europe and the West remains somewhat anomalous. The Turks, who once controlled a quarter of Europe, have a reputation as a race of warriors, and recent decades have shown that violence can still occasionally lie uncomfortably close to the surface in their domestic politics. Three times since 1960 the military have taken over the government. The last time, in 1980, some 20 to 30 people were being killed every day by political extremists on the left and right before the army moved in. In 1983 three political parties were allowed to contest an election, and the Motherland Party came to power with plans to reduce long-standing state controls. They retained their position as the largest party in the Turkish parliament in elections in 1987.

Nazim Hikmet, Turkey's foremost modern poet, expressed in searing verse the sometimes mixed feelings of many of his countrymen about their land:

This country shaped like the head of a mare
Coming full gallop from far-off Asia
To stretch into the Mediterranean:
This country is ours!

Bloody wrists, clenched teeth, bare feet,
Land like a precious silk carpet.
This hell, this paradise is ours.

Hikmet knew better than most. He was imprisoned for 12 years for his radical views, and in 1963 died in exile in Moscow.

Opposite: *A pair of wrestlers sweat on the* göbek tasi *(belly stone) of the* hararet *(hot room) in a Turkish bath in Edirne built by the 16th-century master architect Sinan. Basement boilers produce the steam, and holes in the dome release excess heat. The* hamam, *or Turkish bath, is a direct descendant of the Roman bath, adopted by the Byzantines and then the Ottomans. Steaming is followed by a vigorous rub-down on the hot stone slab. Istanbul still has about 100 public baths, with separate hours or rooms for women. In bygone days, marriage contracts assured wives of their bath allowance.*

Devotees of the nargile *– also known as the water pipe, hookah or hubble-bubble – can still be found puffing away in a leisurely fashion in odd corners of Istanbul. The contraption requires special compressed tobacco and a source of hot cinders to start the slow and delicate process of lighting up. The reward is a peculiarly cool and purified smoke, drawn through water in a glass or crystal vessel. Fine old water pipes are collectors' items.*

The holy warriors

So, just who are the Turks? Once upon a time, so the story goes, a band of 400 horsemen came riding out of the east, and breasting a rise they chanced upon a battle. In a gesture of chivalry, they stormed down the slope to help the losing side, who consequently became the victors. The rescuers were rewarded with a banner, a drum and a small tract of land that they and their valorous descendants expanded into an empire stretching from the gates of Vienna to beyond the Red Sea.

Bir var mis, bir yok mis – 'maybe it happened, maybe it didn't'. That is how Turkish fairy stories start, but here is a legend that bares some relation to the facts. For a thousand years or more, bands of horsemen known as Turks drifted westward out of the arid depths of Central Asia. A hardy, virile people, they travelled light and fast – four horses to a man, for milk and meat as well as for riding – and bred with the daughters of the various tribes they encountered along the way; the result was a vigorous hybrid.

In the 10th century, advancing Turks encountered and embraced Islam, the faith of another nomad people, the Arabs, who three centuries earlier had been galvanised by Muhammad, the Meccan merchant who claimed to have received the word of God – a final clarification of the message of Moses and Jesus. Reacting with the fervour of warrior converts, the Turks soon became the new champions of Islam, carrying it deep into Christianised Asia Minor.

In the midst of these tumultuous times emerged an obscure Turkish clan led by a gazi (holy warrior) named Osman, whose name later became corrupted into English as Ottoman. The Osmanli, or Ottomans, were consigned to the western marches of Turkish territory, on a patch of land granted – if the legend is anything to go by – for services rendered in a clash with the Mongols, another Asiatic horde harrying in the Turkish wake. Combining valour with opportunistic alliances and dynastic marriages, the Ottomans extended their little domain. The 400 horsemen became 4000 by 1300. Growth thereafter was rapid, and achieved by assimilation as much as by conquest. Subjugated communities had only to profess belief in One God, and in Muhammad as His messenger, in order to pass muster as Muslims, and were encouraged to do so by a tax on unbelievers. The Ottomans also stiffened their army with youthful conscripts hand-picked from captured Christian provinces and trained as an élite corps. These janissaries (yeniçeri, or 'new troops') were soon the terror of Europe. Some among them became generals and vezirs (ministers), and in the case of Sinan, the greatest Ottoman architect.

Within little more than a century, the Ottomans had struck deep into the Balkans and completely encircled the eastern capital of Christendom, Constantinople. Founded by Greece in the 7th century BC, and originally called Byzantium, the city became the New Rome of the Emperor Constantine in AD 330, and for centuries after Rome fell to the barbarians it was a world focus of civilisation and wealth. 'From every province of Europe and Asia,' wrote Gibbon, 'the rivulets of gold and silver discharged into the Imperial reservoir a copious and perennial stream.' Its location astride the Bosporus was superb. This, and 13 miles of massive walls and 50 fortified gates, made it a self-contained fortress, with grain reserves and cisterns to sustain it through sieges.

When a crusade, its army composed largely of

The carpets point the way to Mecca – precisely identified by the shell-like niche known as the mihrab. Turks claim to be the originators of the knotted pile carpet. They certainly originated the monumental domed mosque – basing it on a Christian Byzantine model.

Peasant women like these who flock with their families to Istanbul are a world apart from their sophisticated urban sisters, but 99 per cent of Turks are at least nominally Muslim. Bound by a secular constitution, the government tries to fight fundamentalist tendencies while supporting everyone's right to practise a faith.

Traditional water-sellers are still to be found around the Grand Bazaar in Istanbul. Turks are connoisseurs of memba suya, *spring water; they can often tell the source from one sip. Tap water in Istanbul tends to have a bad reputation.*

Part of the pleasure of a shoeshine is the inevitable discussion of yesterday's football match or the next lottery. In the heat of debate it often becomes unclear whose shoes are being shined. Boyaci *– shoeshine men – play an important role in a city where even a poor man prepares for a Sunday outing with a clean suit and a shine.*

December 26, 537. In the 19th century the American writer Mark Twain was rather less ecstatic, dismissing it as 'the rustiest old barn in heathendom'. Most modern visitors would probably incline more towards Justinian's view. St Sophia – Hagia Sophia, 'Divine Wisdom', in Greek – is quite simply a technological marvel that casts ridicule upon the term 'Dark Ages'. Its dome soars the equivalent of 15 storeys and was already a thousand years old when it served as inspiration for Sinan. Emptied long ago of its gold and glitter, St Sophia lies in holy limbo as the great museum-temple of monotheism, its bronze doors opening on to an awesome cavern of subdued golden light that hushes even the most insensitive sightseer.

A five-minute stroll from St Sophia will take in the jumbled core of successive empires – the Roman Hippodrome, the Ottoman Blue Mosque, and the subterranean Byzantine cistern supported by hundreds of columns filched from scores of pagan Greek temples. Of these the Blue Mosque is probably the easiest to recognise because of its six minarets, instead of the usual two or four. This abundance of minarets caused problems for its builder Sultan Ahmed at the beginning of the 17th century, since until then the only other mosque with six minarets had been at Mecca. In the end a storm of protest from various Muslim leaders

Sweet fruit juices are a favourite of the young customers of Turkey's ubiquitous büfe *– snack stands. They come in unusual flavours such as* visne *(sour cherry),* kayisi *(apricot) and* seftali *(peach), as well as the worldwide favourite,* limonata.

Hungarian troops, set forth in 1444 to deal with the Turks, it got no farther than Varna on the Black Sea before being wiped out. Constantinople had sustained a good 50 years of encirclement, and on May 29, 1453, with enormous cannons dragged from Edirne, the janissaries broke through to fulfil a prophecy of the Prophet Muhammad himself. Rude nomads no more, the Ottomans were a major world power.

'Solomon, I have surpassed you!'

Heavy traffic pours through the Edirne Kapi, the Edirne Gate, through which Mehmet the Conqueror entered on a white charger, wearing a royal turban and sky-blue boots, with a rose in his hand, and shouting, 'Halt not the conquerors! God be praised! We are the conquerors!' Setting an itinerary followed by tourists to this day, the sultan rode directly to St Sophia, the greatest church in all Christendom, and ordered no more desecration than was necessary to convert it into a mosque. Thus it is that today a Christian-style basilica with minarets serenely crowns the Istanbul skyline.

'Solomon, I have surpassed you!' the Emperor Justinian is said to have cried upon its consecration on

Brightly decorated carts – once a feature of Turkey – are to be seen only around Edirne and parts of the Anatolian coast. But the roads are no less cheerful, for many trucks now receive the same treatment. Some are real works of art.

prompted the Sultan to get around the problem by sending his architect post-haste to Mecca to add a seventh minaret to the mosque there.

At the limit of land, meanwhile, where Seraglio Point pushes like the prow of a ship into the Bosporus, with the Sea of Marmara to starboard and the Golden Horn to port, are the pavilions, kiosks, courtyards, follies and fountains of Topkapi Sarayi, the fabulous palace of the sultans. For 400 years, this was the nerve centre of the Ottoman Empire and of Islam itself, for the sultans also claimed the title of *Caliph* (successor of Muhammad and spiritual leader of Islam) as well as those of Commander of the Faithful and Shadow of God on earth. The palace's heart is the harem (meaning 'forbidden' in Arabic), a warren of more than 300 rooms, baths and courtyards, once the most inaccessible

Gypsies have been bringing performing bears to Istanbul and other Turkish towns since the Middle Ages, but the World Wildlife Fund hopes to end the practice by buying off the owners. The bears `perform' by being harnessed in a way that forces them on to their hind legs for days on end.

building on earth and now tramped by tour groups daily between ten o'clock and four.

This is where the tremendous energy of the early Ottomans was dissipated by self-indulgence; where some sultans spent more money on beautifying their already spectacular home than on the whole of the rest of their empire; and where the murderous intrigues of eunuch, favourite and *valide sultan* (the sultan's mother, always a power behind the throne) rotted the empire from the core. Sultans with names such as Conqueror, Thunderbolt and Magnificent were succeeded by the likes of Selim the Sot, Ibrahim the Mad (who once, in a fit of pique, drowned 279 concubines in the Bosporus) and the paranoid Abdul the Damned, who ended his days trusting only a cat for company.

Istanbul has a pigeon problem, but don't tell that to the citizens who spend precious lira on little dishes of birdseed near the Beyazit Mosque. The story goes that the birds are descended from a pair donated by a pious woman hundreds of years ago, and that you gain a little spiritual reward by feeding them. Besides, Turks are fond of pigeons.

Under the magic skyline

A breezy refrain from an old popular song records Constantinople's change of name to Istanbul in 1926.

Why did Constantinople get the works?
It's nobody's business but the Turks' . . .

Coming from the Byzantine Greek phrase '*eis ten polin*' meaning 'in the city', or 'to the city', Istanbul had been in everyday use for many centuries, but its formal adoption was part of a bid to exorcise the past and to make a new beginning. Nowadays it is only the Greeks who, to vex the Turks, persist in calling it Constantinople.

It takes more than a change of name to subdue such a past, however. Seven decades after its loss of title, the city of 89 emperors and 30 sultans remains the mercantile and cultural capital of Turkey, the focus of

Love letters, job applications, government forms . . . the street scribe near the Spice Market puts into words what his unlettered clients cannot express for themselves. Once common, there are fewer of his kind about.

more than half Turkey's industry. Its population has soared from 1.8 million in 1960 to more than 7 million today. A large majority are first-generation arrivals from rural Anatolia, and another quarter-million arrive each year, straining the planners' attempts to make modern sense out of ancient attitudes and habit. 'Traffic in Istanbul moves like herds of sheep', laments one urban planner. 'They drive cars, but treat them like horses!' *Gecekondu* shanty towns clog the outskirts and any available space, gradually improved into real neighbourhoods by their resourceful inhabitants. It has been calculated that Istanbul has 40 times less green space per head than Stockholm.

Services such as electricity are stretched beyond their limits. Streets that were originally constructed for pedestrians and pack animals now crumble under the weight of hundreds of thousands of cars, trucks and buses. In summer, dust tracks pass for pavements, whilst later in the year, slurried mud obscures treacherous pits. In winter, the magic skyline disappears under fog charged with fumes from the lignite that heats the city; in spring, it re-emerges . . . under a fresh cloak of soot. The climate, too, can be treacherous. In winter the prevailing north-east wind or *poyraz*, blowing in off the Black Sea, will shift suddenly to the north-east becoming the so-called *karayel*, or 'black veil'. This sends in icy draughts from the mountains of the Balkans and is so cold that the Golden Horn and even parts of the Bosporus sometimes freeze over. At other times of the year, the *lodos* or south-west wind is the danger, blowing up sudden storms on the Sea of Marmara.

Even Istanbul's spectacular and strategic setting presents problems, for it is built – like the original Rome – on seven hills rising from the waterfront. 'How can I bring water up such hills?' an exasperated mayor once remonstrated. 'How can I build roads? How can I collect the refuse?' Two suspension bridges spanning the mile-wide Bosporus were supposed to relieve congestion, but they only worsened it by stimulating long-distance trucking and generating a jam of juggernauts – and thus further urban sprawl.

The Golden Horn, meanwhile, is golden only in the mind's eye, or under a kindly sunset: the fabled and once-lovely anchorage became a dump for the worst of the city's pollution, and has only gradually responded to clean-up efforts. None the less, it is still a focus for the city's life. At the Galata Bridge over the Horn, all Turkey comes together in a cacophony of hoots and whistles, the cries of pedlars mixing with the grunts of *hamal,* porters bearing tremendous loads of merchandise. Foreheads sticky and dirty with sweat, bent double under twice their weight, the *hamal* have achieved this at least: they are in Istanbul.

Across the Horn

Across the Galata Bridge is Beyoglu, formerly Pera (meaning 'over there'). This is the old European quarter, once legendary for the excesses and intrigues of its cosmopolitan society. Here is where power came to reside in the 19th century, upon the heights between the

Opposite: *Fishermen take the direct approach in trying to interest buyers on the quay at Üsküdar, on the Asiatic side of the Bosporus. This was once the starting point for the annual Sacred Caravan to Mecca. Now it is a shopping centre for a fast-expanding urban area that enjoys sea breezes and superb views of old Istanbul.*

The fare is so fresh that flapping fish play havoc with the decorative displays at this waterfront restaurant. Diners make their own selection, then retire to await results at one of the tables behind the display. This pleasant aspect of Istanbul life so delighted an Austrian ambassador to the Ottoman court that he brought the idea of the open-air café back to Europe.

Blessed with the blithe unconcern of youth, this cheerful Anatolian girl is typical of so many who come to Istanbul with their families. The Covered Bazaar provides a multitude of small jobs for such youngsters.

Horn and the Bosporus, and this is the direction of the modern city's growth. The dilapidated former Grand Rue of long-redundant embassies has become a pedestrian mall threading up to Taksim Square, the hub of modern Istanbul. A gigantic open space with bland modern architecture, Taksim Square gives access to the international hotels and haunts of the *entel* (from entelektuel, the fashionable set), to the bar-restaurants, discos and fashionable suburbs that are almost not Turkish at all, except for the way wealth is displayed with such a fine, grave swagger.

A nightclub now sits on top of the Galata Tower, which was built by the Genoese in 1348 and was once known as the Tower of Christ. Refurbishers have restored the Pera Palas hotel to Edwardian elegance, and tour buses drop their passengers at Cicek (Flower) Pasaji, the alley where Turkish bohemia has traditionally cavorted; but it takes more than a little urban renewal and genteel tourism to subdue such a past.

'The tunes are soft, the motions so languishing', wrote Lady Mary Wortley Montagu of Pera's belly dancers in the 18th century. They are less languishing now, perhaps, but no less lubricious, as countless modern practitioners of the art do their bit for a nightlife that tries to be worthy of the quarter's spicier traditions. Casanova spent the summer of 1744 in Pera, and in his memoirs the great lover admits to being seduced only once – and then by a gentleman named Ismail. The number of transvestites hereabouts may suggest an explanation for this lapse.

Beyond Beyoglu to the north you reach some of the lovely and still remarkably unspoilt towns and villages lining the Bosporus, where Istanbul's wealthier citizens have traditionally retreated in summer. The Bosporus itself can be dangerous at this point with treacherous cross-currents swirling through the narrow channel. But the scenery rising from the shores on either side could hardly be more serene. Villages such as Arnavütkoy and

Shopping for a Turkish carpet or flat-weave kilim *in the Grand Bazaar is a challenging adventure, with the selection virtually limitless and haggling expected. Machine-made imitations abound and collectors' items are increasingly hard to find, but fine carpets continue to be woven on village and nomad looms by mother-and-daughter teams using techniques handed down through many centuries.*

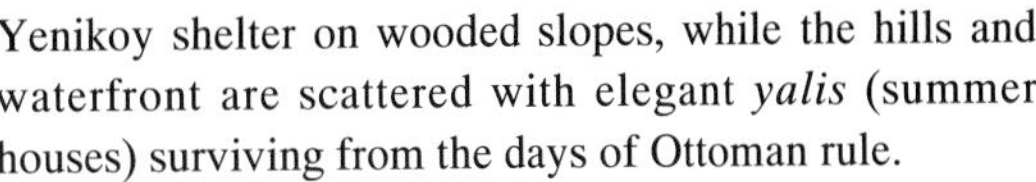

Yenikoy shelter on wooded slopes, while the hills and waterfront are scattered with elegant *yalis* (summer houses) surviving from the days of Ottoman rule.

This street of jewellers in the Grand Covered Bazaar covers the spectrum from tourist trinket to precious heirloom. Most dealers speak several languages, and bargaining calls for patience and the inevitable glass of tea. The reddish hue of the necklaces displayed in the foreground is an effect that Istanbul goldsmiths obtain by mixing copper with gold.

The biggest bazaar in the world

Back in Istanbul, the Kapali Carsi, or Grand Covered Bazaar, was given a military shake-up – like the rest of Turkey – after the 1980 army coup. Everything you could possibly want to buy is neatly stacked somewhere in this ancestor of the modern shopping centre, which boasts of having the world's largest concentration of shops and stalls under one roof. Here, in the heart of old

Istanbul, under 50 acres of domed and vaulted ceiling accumulated over 500 years, is the total Turkish experience. This was the first thing that Mehmet built when he had to pump life back into the conquered city, and it remains today a great cauldron of commerce.

In 1880, a survey found the Grand Bazaar to contain 7491 shops, stalls and craft workshops, 12 storehouses, 18 fountains, 12 mescit (small mosques), one large mosque, a school and a tomb – to which today could be added half a dozen restaurants, countless teashops and cafés, two banks, a police station, a post office and a tourist information centre. What feels like a labyrinth was planned on a grid system, each of the 67 streets known by the guild that once operated it. Thus you will still find Carpet-sellers Street, the Avenue of the Slippers, and the Street of the Pearl Merchants . . .

It is hardly surprising that there is a Street of the Mirrormakers, for the Turkish male is often to be seen regarding his reflection in a street window. Stoutness here is nothing to be ashamed about, being a symbol of success. This is just as well, when one considers Turkish cuisine. The original Turkish horsemen brought with them yoghurt and a way of roasting meat on spits or skewers over their camp fires – the now universal kebab. A few hundred years of epicurean adaptation to Mediterranean living did the rest. The result is a kind of Topkapi of cuisines, ranging from a bewildering array of *meze* (appetisers) to honey-and-syrup-soaked confections with names such as Lady's Navel and Lips of the Beloved – and, of course, Turkish Delight. Few countries offer more eating options. At dawn in the older residential quarters of Istanbul you are still sometimes woken by the cry of the *simit*-seller walking through the streets carrying small hoop-like rolls covered with sesame seeds. At the same time, stacks of flaky börek pastries stuffed with meat or cheese are laid out in wait for early morning workers, and from then on snacks and delicacies assail the senses at every street corner, the aromas issuing from carts and *bufes* (small stalls), kebab and *pide* (Turkish pitta bread), *kafeteria,* soup kitchens, pudding shops and *lokantas* (restaurants). Even the dives called *meyhane* are capable of serving surprising delicacies to *raki* drinkers, imbibers of the aniseed-based national drink.

Four hundred thousand people surge and drift through the Grand Bazaar on a busy Saturday, yet its surprises include quiet places. Beyond the Street of the Pearl Merchants, the 16th-century Sandal Bedesten is a lofty hall of brick domes and dim light, with what would appear to be all the carpets of Turkey stacked in mounds, waiting to be auctioned. A right turn from here and then a left takes the shopper suddenly into a mosque courtyard, shaded by chestnuts and plane trees; for company, there is always a colourful collection of beggars and pedlars, and sometimes an *asik*, a wandering Anatolian minstrel. The Grand Bazaar has no clear ending, but spills into the surrounding districts through dozens of *han,* Ottoman inns or caravanserais, where the merchants with their caravans used to rest and do business. A number of the *hans* have been rebuilt in recent years, but many of the picturesque old ones survive. They often have tree-shaded cobbled yards and harbour workshops and warehouses, forges and craft factories, and still more shops.

The opium poppy is native to Turkey, which was once the major source of illicit heroin-smuggling into Western countries. Since 1975, the crop has been under tight State control to ensure that it goes only to legal users, such as the manufacturers of pain-killing medicines.

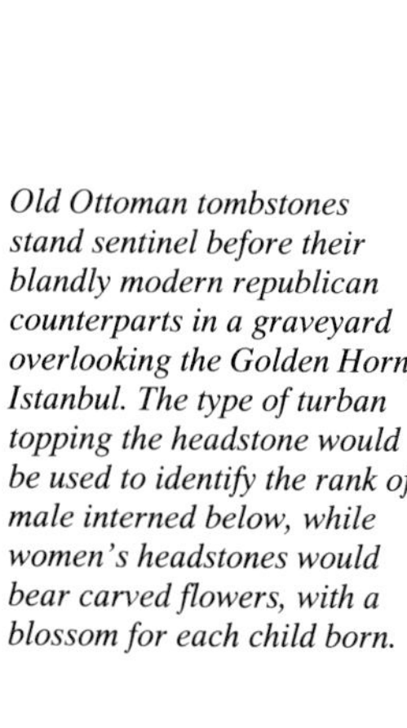

Old Ottoman tombstones stand sentinel before their blandly modern republican counterparts in a graveyard overlooking the Golden Horn, Istanbul. The type of turban topping the headstone would be used to identify the rank of male interned below, while women's headstones would bear carved flowers, with a blossom for each child born.

Anatolia: The Turkish Sunrise

You can take the bus to Anatolia now that the Bosporus is bridged, but a better way is by ferry, a 15-minute voyage of discovery from Europe to Asia. Bells clang and spoons clink in little tea glasses wielded by *efendi,* cultured urban commuters engrossed in their newspapers, or proffered to the diffident foreigner by some shabbily dressed country *koylu,* whose dour demeanour cloaks cordiality worthy of an Ottoman prince. It is virtually impossible to be anywhere in Turkey for 15 minutes without being offered tea.

Anatolia – from the Greek, signifying 'sunrise' – is also known as Asia Minor. It is a squat extrusion of the Asian continent, almost 1000 miles from west to east and 500 from north to south. It is broken and mountainous, with earthquakes a constant threat. Climbing away from the coast are mountain ramparts – the Pontus Mountains in the north and the Taurus Mountains in the south – that hide an interior akin to the steppes of Russia: a plateau worn and torn by a criss-cross of contesting peoples since before the dawn of history. This is Turkey's granary, producing crops of cereals, rice, cotton, fruit and tobacco, yet it is also still untamed enough for the shepherd dogs to wear spiked iron collars as protection against wolves.

Dust storms choke the hot Anatolian summers, while winters bring snowstorms that seal off villages, isolated at the best of times. The snow lies deeper and longer as the plateau tilts upwards towards the east, where temperatures in the mountains can plunge up to 40° below zero. They call this Turkey's Siberia, and in January 1915 at the battle of Sarikamis, 30,000 soldiers died when their commander attempted an overly ambitious manoeuvre in a blizzard. When it comes, spring is a joyous release of endless meadows of grass and wild flowers nourished by the snow melt.

Tucked into Anatolia's north-eastern corner, meanwhile, is the fabled port city of Trabzon (or Trebizond), wedged between the Pontus Mountains and the Black Sea. Here from the early 13th century the wily dynasty of the Grand Comneni, an offshoot of the Byzantine imperial family, held sway until in 1461 the last emperor, David Comnenus, was obliged to surrender to overwhelming forces under Sultan Mehmet, Constantinople's conqueror. In its heyday Trabzon was a place of fabulous wealth, a key stopping place on the trade routes across the Black Sea and Asia Minor and famous for the skills of its craftsmen in silver and iron and its weavers, and for the production of an

A camel and its support team wait to do battle. Camel wrestling is a popular winter sport in south-eastern Turkey. The beasts are force-fed throughout the summer to increase their weight and shorten their temper. They are muzzled to prevent biting; if serious damage threatens, the camels are hauled apart. The contest is a clumsy ballet in slow motion. There is heavy betting on the outcome, and all-night celebrations with music and rounds of raki *afterwards.*

Fat-bellied caiques rock at their moorings while their skippers relax at a quayside kahve *and count the sheep passing by. Despite the transformation of the Aegean by tourism, there is more than enough jagged, indented coastline to protect fishing ports such as this one from the attention of the crowds.*

inky black wine. Something of that exotic appeal still clings to the modern city (whose other claim to fame is one of Turkey's best-known football teams). Its bazaar is still large and colourful, while the Kale (old town) looks as formidable as ever, spread over a rocky ledge with a plunging ravine on either side. And about a mile outside the Kale is the Aya Sofia (Hagia Sophia) Church, built in 1245 by the Emperor Manuel Comnenus, with some of the most beautiful of all late Byzantine frescoes. Rising in the twilight of the central dome and barrel-vaulted roofs are astonishingly fresh depictions of the miracles of Jesus, the Virgin Mary taking her place in Heaven and, in the porch, lurid fragments from the Last Judgement – including one of a wolf gobbling up lost souls.

This whole environment of contrasts has worked itself into the character of the people of Anatolia as a fusion of extremes. 'We find them brave and pusillanimous, gentle and ferocious, active and indolent . . . at once delicate and coarse', wrote one British merchant more than a century ago. The word *misafir* – guest – has an almost sacred connotation in Anatolia, as the stranded

motorist discovers when royally received in some villager's *misafir odasi* (guest room). But woe betide the stranger who makes a remark that is taken to be a slight or, worst of all, a criticism of their country, even in jest.

What Father did to the Turks

Turks are touchy with reason. Anatolia is their homeland, but only this century was it secured as such, and by the will of one man, who now lies buried at its heart in a massive tomb like a pagan temple. They honoured him with the name Atatürk – Father of the Turks. As Mustafa Kemal Pasha he was the last Ottoman war hero, who offered defiance (by successfully defending Gallipoli) when the Allies rolled over what was left of the bankrupt empire to share it out piecemeal at the conclusion of the First World War. In two years of further fighting, he led a ragtag rebel force to victory over a Greek army occupying western Anatolia, and grabbed back what else he could.

To complete the job, Atatürk took it upon himself to give the Turks a new identity, one in which nationalism replaced Islam as the moving force. Islam was tolerated as a religion, but little more, and traditions of 500 years were abolished. Westernisation was enforced, even in matters of dress. The veil was denounced as a barbarous relic, and the fez outlawed as 'an emblem of ignorance'. The Swiss civil code was adapted to Turkish conditions; polygamy was outlawed, and women given the vote. Everyone was obliged to have a surname. Sunday replaced the Muslim Friday as the day of rest. The old Arabic script was replaced with a modified version of the Roman alphabet, its letters closely reflecting the sounds of spoken Turkish, so that it could be taught more easily to the illiterate masses. At the same time, attempts were made to purge the muscular Turkish tongue of words of Arabic or Persian origin and to replace them with 'pure Turkish' words, sometimes newly invented for the purpose. 'Call yourself a Turk and be proud of it', the liberator ordered.

Although he has been dead more than 50 years, Atatürk continues to watch over the Türkiye – 'Land of the Turks' – he created. His statue commands every village square, every shop, every hotel foyer; he looks out from the coins and banknotes; he gazes down from

Sponge diving has been marginalised by tourism in Bodrum, but remains the major activity of a few coastal villages. Improved equipment has not lessened the danger, for the divers venture deeper and take chances with bad weather conditions. An unexpected beneficiary has been the exciting new science of underwater archaeology. The divers have located several ancient wrecks, including the most ancient found anywhere – a richly laden trading vessel of 1400 BC.

Groups of men whiling away the afternoons like this may be found throughout the country. They sip tea, smoke, play cards and sip more tea. Turkish coffee is reserved for special occasions due to its expense: it is one of the few crops Turkey does not grow.

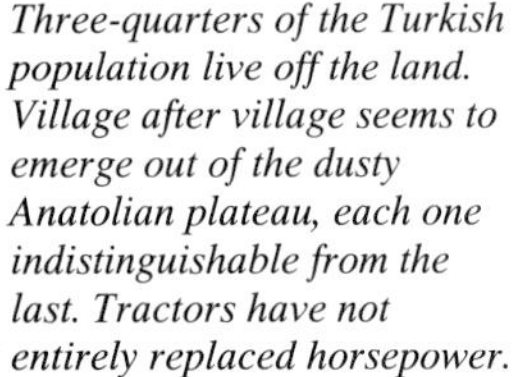

Three-quarters of the Turkish population live off the land. Village after village seems to emerge out of the dusty Anatolian plateau, each one indistinguishable from the last. Tractors have not entirely replaced horsepower.

banners that drape entire buildings, his cold blue eyes and red hair a singular comment upon just how hybrid a Turk can be. The tomb that took ten years to build is the last thing Turks see on their television each night. It stands on a hill overlooking the capital, Ankara.

The prospect below is of traffic charging along wide thoroughfares, horns blaring, scattering pedestrians like the flocks of Angora goats that were a point of pride before Atatürk chose to base his revolution here. Modern Ankara is a glass and concrete aggregation with the worst air pollution in Turkey, but also the most energy. The population of more than 3 million grows by the day. Under customary law, a man may not be dispossessed if, overnight, he can put a roof on four walls. Hence the *gecekondu* squatter villages oozing up and over the hillsides.

But across the valley, beyond the railway tracks, there is another Ankara, a place of narrow, cobbled streets and ramshackle wooden houses. Perched on a high point that has been occupied for thousands of

years, the old town seems to defy the planners in their skyscrapers down below. Children fly kites from the battlements, and women in baggy *salvar* trousers stand in doorways gossiping, while in a pre-Ottoman mosque next to the bazaar, a *hoca* (religious teacher) with a pointed beard is teaching the Koran to a group of small boys clad in jeans and sitting cross-legged on rugs. A long finger admonishes, and the boys sway back and forth, chanting in Arabic, setting to memory words they cannot understand, just as it was before Atatürk.

The Turquoise Coast

In Turkey, the old ways are only a turn, a few miles at most, off the fine new roads. This is true even of Bodrum, in its cupped cove in the crook of the ancient classical world, where the Turquoise Coast of the travel agents (otherwise known as the Mediterranean) begins to bend away from the Aegean. Bodrum used to be locked into antiquity, a community of sponge divers with boats cosily drawn up around the little mosque, and a Crusader castle standing guard a polite distance away. Then, in the wake of the Atatürk reforms, Bodrum began to attract artists and bohemians. 'When the moon comes up, the universe turns into a fairy tale', one of them wrote in the 1930s. Now it turns into a discotheque, shooting laser beams at the castle, for Bodrum has become an international yachting mecca, a hedonistic sun trap sometimes referred to as 'Bedroom' by the disrespectful. The tall masts of the foreign yachts crowd out the minarets by the sea, the little mosque jostled by piano and jazz bars, boutiques and rug shops; in Bodrum, they will even run you up a rug portrait.

This traditional house style features a cumba, an upper-floor room with an overhanging casement in which the women relax, sew, chatter and eye the passers-by.

But explore Bodrum carefully, and it becomes apparent how much of the past still survives, if more affluently now – from the traditional sandal maker, now with a clientele of famous names, yet hardly changed in his ways, to the skipper who runs charters along the coast in a boat that required a sheep sacrifice for its launch. On Sundays when the tourists are mostly gone, café tables in the village square are placed under the trees for an event of great joy to parents, but of anxiety to the small boys who must undergo, in public, their circumcision. Before the ceremony the boys are blessed at the mosque, and driven in triumph through the narrow streets, car horns honking. Then the boys to be circumcised are held standing on a table with pants down, while the operation is performed. It has been drummed into the children that they are about to become men, and must on no account cry – or scream – and parents have been known to stuff a boy's mouth with chocolate in a desperate ploy to stifle the sobs.

Tourist Turkey marches inexorably eastward with each season, planting dazzling white hotels like marker buoys along a coast now served by three international airports, bringing bounty – and pollution – to every fishing village that can boast a sandy beach and tumbled temple. Side, where Mark Antony wooed Cleopatra, lay forgotten for a millennium, the prey of marauding Arabs and earthquakes, until local fishermen set up a lemonade shack, then a bar, then another, amidst the archaeology; now Side has hotel accommodation for as many as its amphitheatre once accommodated – 25,000.

Atatürk ordered his people into Western clothes as a sign of modern thinking. The loose, baggy salvar *trousers of village women are one traditional item to survive, whilst the wraparound headscarf is a conservative solution to Atatürk's condemnation of the veil. The black bouffant pants of the man have become a rare sight, even here in eastern Anatolia.*

The Whirling Dervishes

If Ankara and the Turquoise Coast exemplify the new Turkey, Konya is a shrine to tradition and continuity: a place of pilgrimage and a centre of Sufi mysticism. Sufism arose as an early reaction against what today would be called Islamic fundamentalism, and its most joyous exponent was the man who became Konya's 'patron saint', the poet Celaleddin Rumi, known to Turks as the *Mevlana* – the Master. Rumi welcomed all faiths (Sufis consider Christ to be a Sufi) and trampled on dogma by stressing the equality of men and women and advocating music and dancing as ways to a higher understanding of the divine. 'Ultimate truth is reached by love', was one of his messages. After his death on December 17, 1273, his Mevlevi followers formed a mystic order, the Mevlevi, better known as the Whirling Dervishes, after their sacred dance. The order was sustained for 650 years until banned by Atatürk.

A fluted tower hovers over the Mevlana's *turbe* (tomb) in the finest surviving *tekke* (Dervish monastery) in Turkey; it acts as a beacon for the pilgrims who flock here, some to stay for eternity. To be buried close to a saint is a step towards paradise, and so the tomb is attended by a shady, inviting graveyard. Atatürk's strictures still stand; as a result, the monastery is technically a museum, and pilgrims must queue with the tourists at a ticket window. But this in no way diminishes the intensity of their experience before the sarcophagus, draped with green and red silk.

The tall white turban at its head gives the impression that Rumi himself is standing there, as he surely is to the devout line that shuffles forward, to kneel and kiss the railing of the catafalque, and murmur a greeting – *'Selamunaleykum'*. Softly from above comes the poignant, lonely sound of a flute, in conscious echo of the Mevlana's poetry:

Day and night, music,
A quiet, bright reed song.
If it fades, we fade

When tour groups burst in, the spell is cruelly broken.

Cappadocia's haunted moonscape

Beyond Konya lies Cappadocia, where a record of human piety and perseverance is literally carved into the landscape. Cappadocia is a geological joke, a fierce prank of nature to relieve the monotony of the treeless

Turks take intense pride in the product of their labours, whether it is the bread of this baker, or a simple shoeshine.

This couple will remain at the market for as long as it takes to dispose of their small stock. The family budget would collapse otherwise.

The many markets set the rhythm of life in the southern countryside. The men make for the café; the women enjoy the opportunity for gossip while selling their handicrafts and making a selection from bolts of brightly patterned cotton cloth.

plain. Volcanic eruptions long ago smothered much of the area under a thick layer of tufa, a soft rock formed from compressed ash, stirred in with lumps of hard basalt. Weathering created a surrealistic moonscape of stark ravines and crazy cones, so soft that for thousands of years man gouged out dwellings: crude caves at first, but eventually accommodation for whole communities. Deep gulleys hide the entrances to the underground cities: chilly even in the height of summer, fearful in their claustrophobia, and descending through more than a dozen levels.

Early Christians settled here, scooping out hermits' cells, monastery warrens and churches; some are small cathedrals, with domes, vaults, arches and pillars hewn

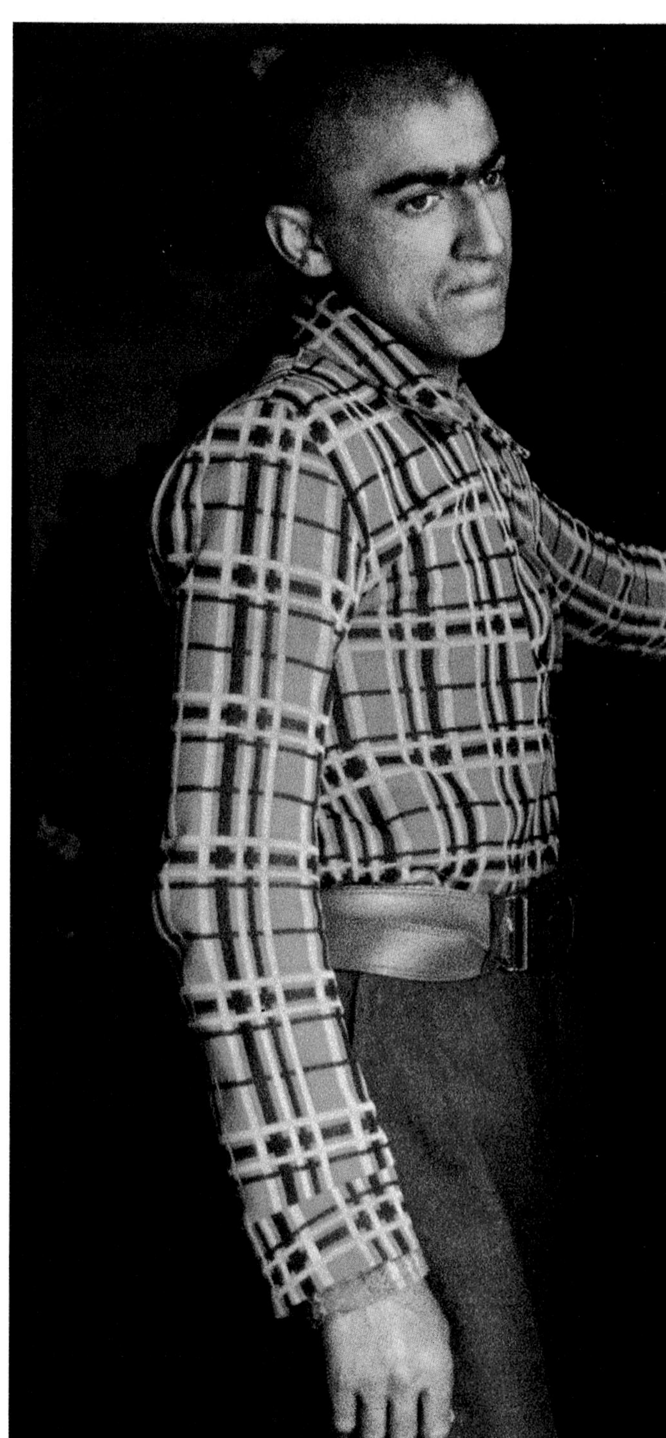

out of the living rock and decorated with elaborate, colourful frescoes from an age when saints and miracles were in peculiar abundance. Images of St George are particularly numerous, trampling and skewering serpent-dragons in the eternal twilight: a surprise, perhaps, until one learns that Cappadocia was the birthplace of England's patron saint.

The Christians are all gone, the last only in 1925, in the wrenching exchange of populations with Greece that was part of the birth of modern Turkey, but a rustic piety endures in the mingling of the *muezzins'* call with the dawn chorus of braying donkeys. Robust, hospitable and respectful of tradition, the Cappadocians live as they always have. The volcanic dust looks deathly, but is wonderfully fertile, and the weird ravines are permeated with orchards, vegetable gardens and vineyards. Here and there people still occupy a rock dwelling, a cat at the little door or a geranium in the window, lending it a fairy-tale quality. In others, they

The thread which is being hand-spun at Siverek in central Anatolia will be treated with dyes made from madder root, indigo, walnut, saffron and other native plants. Turkey has several schemes to encourage the use of the natural dyes and traditional designs prized by collectors. Chemical colours cannot match the luminous subtlety of the natural tones, but villagers have a taste for their brightness.

This Konyan coppersmith is putting the finishing touches to the kind of tray on which meals are traditionally served in Turkish homes. Since copper is mildly toxic, the interior surface is sometimes given a tin layer. The apprentice will spend years learning how to beat, cut and embellish trays, pots, pans and all manner of other items. Turkey's master craftsmen are experts in making new objects look like antiques.

store plums and apricots, wheat, chickens and donkeys – and the occasional motor car.

Off the tufa, across flat fields of sunflowers (which the Turks call moonflowers), the hubbub and the smells of sheepskin and raw silk, herbs and spices exuding from the markets of Kayseri must be much as Xenophon would have known them. The best rugs and wool in Turkey are traded here in vaulted markets and *hans* under the walls of a citadel buffeted by Romans, Arabs, Crusaders, Mongols and Turks, and now in useful retirement as a shopping precinct.

Fast and sacrifice

Despite continued attachment to Atatürk's revolution, Turkish secularists have come to accept Islam's role in national life, although they worry that in recent years as many mosques as schools may have been built. The estimated total is 65,000 – a mosque for every 800 citizens – and on Fridays they tend to be full, whereas in the reformist 1930s they were almost empty, at least in the cities. In the Anatolian countryside, it was never a contest. Islam sets the pulse of life, doing away with the need for clocks as five times in every 24 hours – at dawn, midday, mid-afternoon, sunset and nightfall – the *muezzin* in the minaret calls the times of prayer.

The fine balance between secular values and Islamic sensibilities is probably best in evidence during Ramadan (*Ramazan* in Turkish), the holy month when Muslims are supposed to fast from dawn to dusk. Many restaurants and cafés close throughout the day, especially in Anatolia's conservative heartland, but some elect to operate with curtains discreetly drawn, and tourist resorts carry on as usual.

Drumbeats before dawn rouse people in time to enjoy a last meal before the new day's fast begins. At the end of the day, a cannon boom ends the fast, triggering a stampede to shops, restaurants and teahouses, while lines form at bakeries to buy hot and spicy *Ramazan* bread for the lavish meals prepared in every home. *Ramazan* ends with the *Seker Bayrami* (Sugar Holiday), three days of hectic partying, with gifts for the children.

Two months later, there is the *Kurban Bayrami* (Festival of the Sacrifice) which can be somewhat startling to Western eyes. Towns and cities become clogged with sheep that are trucked in from all over Anatolia and are bought on street corners by every household able to afford one. On the appointed morning, some 2.5 million animals have their throats cut in individual re-enactments of the Koranic version of the Biblical story of Abraham's sacrifice to God. Families keep what they need and donate the rest of the meat, the skin and the fleece to the poor, so that the entire country may enjoy the three days of celebrations that follow.

The roof of Turkey

The diesel-spewing trucks and buses thundering eastwards from Istanbul and Ankara make a racetrack of the ancient trade and invasion route across Anatolia – until, of course, they are brought to a grinding crawl by some farmer on his tractor, with his family hunched into a trailing cart. The farmer does not get of the way – he does not even look round – but stays steadfastly on his creeping course.

Eastern Anatolia is like this: obdurate, refusing to be bullied by bureaucrats striving after the goals of Atatürk. Poverty closes in with the weather, with each mile travelled. Endurance is the trait most essential for life on the chill, eroded roof of the steppe around Erzurum, Turkey's highest, most exposed, most

Turkey supplies two-thirds of the world's hazelnuts; here is a portion of the crop being dried. Women have a subordinate role in rural Turkish life, but not when it comes to work in the fields. The mechanisation of agriculture has eased their burden, but some tasks still have to be done by hand. The hazel tree was sacred in ancient times and many cultures imbue it with mystic powers, in water divining, for instance. Turks say the hazel grew in the Garden of Eden; the Romans burned it for good luck at weddings; and Arab tradition holds it to be a protection against evil.

The medieval town of Konya is a last stronghold of Muslim mysticism in Turkey, and the site each December of a popular Dervish festival. Under a watchful government eye, Dervish sects are reviving as part of the Islamic resurgence.

Like human spinning tops, Dervishes whirl in great circles that induce a trance-like state. The object is to seek union with God, with each motion and gesture having a religious significance. The upturned right palm and the downturned left create a spiritual lightning rod along which grace flows from heaven to earth. The conical camel-hair hat represents a tombstone; the white skirt is a shroud; and a black cloak cast aside in the course of the ceremony is the tomb itself: a symbol of the earthly bondage from which the dance offers deliverance. Adepts attain supreme dexterity and powers of endurance through years of practice.

earthquake-prone and probably most conservative city. Villages burrow into the earth for protection from the harsh, six-month winter. Their inhabitants huddle around *tandirs,* stoves fuelled by dried cow dung, dug into the ground beneath heat-containing platforms covered by pretty kilim rugs. At night, upwards of a dozen people will sleep, toes to the *tandir,* on a circle of mattresses. Outside, new village mosques keep appearing between the hayricks and pyramids of dried dung. Awkward parodies of traditional styles, with flashy factory-made tiles, they are privately financed by *vakifs,* religious endowments that rely mainly upon donations from Saudi Arabia.

Presenting a more smiling face is Lake Van, Turkey's largest lake covering over 1400 square miles. But this too has its quirks. At first sight its dark green waters seem normal enough . . . but then you notice something strange about the way they move. Instead of forming crested waves, they billow out in smooth, slightly oily ripples, rather as if someone were shaking a piece of heavy green silk. The truth is that Lake Van is an almost entirely dead sea. When a lava flow oozed its way across the lowlands to the south-west well over 20,000 years ago it blocked the one escape route for the waters gathered in the huge bowl of surrounding mountains. Consequently, water flows into Lake Van, but never out, thus accumulating large concentrations of mineral salts and sulphides. A kind of hardy carp, the darekh, is the only animal that can survive in its waters.

For all that, the region around Lake Van is one of eastern Turkey's most hospitable areas, as well as its most interesting and beautiful. Few darekh fishermen

Cappadocia's lunar landscape results from the weathering of thick volcanic deposits. Its barren appearance is deceptive, for it produces excellent fruit and other crops.

Popularly known as fairy chimneys, these quaintly eroded features of Cappadocia were hollowed out to create human habitations; many are used today as storehouses and granaries.

The harsh Anatolian climate of torrid summers and glacial winters engraves itself into the features of those who have to endure it.

set sail from the lakeside towns any more, but small passenger steamers still ply between them, trailing flocks of screeching, ever-optimistic seagulls hunting for scraps. In winter the whole region is blanketed with thick snow, but at other times of year the gentler slopes and plateaus round about are clothed with fields of rye, flourishing market gardens and orchards of ripening apples. Tourists too are playing an increasingly important part in the local economy, drawn by the spectacular scenery: waterfalls tumbling down rugged mountainsides; the towering peak of Süphan Dagi rising over 13,000 feet above the lake's northern shore.

The people here are alert and friendly – which is not surprising, since they have a proud heritage behind them. The Lake Van region was first settled at least 15,000 years ago, as several cave paintings in the mountains bear witness. Perched on a rocky outcrop above the town of Van, meanwhile, are the remains of an ancient citadel which dates in part from the time of the Urartians who prospered in the 10th to 8th centuries BC. Theirs were evidently a sophisticated civilisation and the museum at Van contains some fine examples of their jewellery and bronzeware.

No less sophisticated, though of more recent date, are the remains on the now uninhabited lake island of Akhtamar. In the 10th and 11th centuries AD the small Armenian kingdom of Vaspurakan spread out around Lake Van, and in 920 its most famous king, Gagik, built himself a palace and a church on the island. Only the foundations of the palace now survive, but the Church of the Holy Cross still stands, a drum-shaped gem in pinkish sandstone. Its chief glories are its marvellous sculptures depicting everything from eagles to guinea fowls, lions to bears. In one corner Adam and Eve are being tempted in the Garden of Eden; in another David is vanquishing Goliath. Jonah falls into the mouth of a rather unlikely looking whale, and in one of the finest of the sculptures Gagik presents himself with his church to Christ.

The simple peasant lifestyle of Cappadocia has miraculously survived the attentions of tourism. Here, tomatoes ripen under a hot morning sun.

Mountain Turks and Noah's Ark

Ne mutlu Turkum diyene! 'Happy is he who calls himself a Turk!' Atatürk's words are carved on walls, monuments, even on mountains throughout Turkey. But the country's mightiest mountain is a reminder of the unspoken corollary: the sometimes unhappy fate of non-Turks. Agri Dagi – Mount Ararat – is one of the world's mystic peaks. This stupendous volcanic cone, perfect enough for a geometry lesson, rears to 16,700 feet, pinioning the border with Armenia and Iran. Certain Christian fundamentalists, including one American astronaut, are convinced that Noah's Ark is still up there somewhere, and mount as many expeditions to try to recover it as the Turks are prepared to tolerate. To Armenians scattered around the world, the appeal is

Preparing and baking the bread is a priority for the women of a typical rural family in eastern Anatolia. With each household making its own, the aroma soon percolates throughout the hamlet. Afterwards, the women will make for the well or fountain to do the laundry, followed by a trail of laughing children.

The pide, *or Turkish pizza bread, which these women are baking will be stuffed with spices, tomatoes and* döner kebap – *crusty slices cut from lamb roasting on a vertical turning spit.* Döner kebap *is the nearest thing to a national dish.*

The beehive mudbrick villages of the Harran plain have been dying from lack of water, with most of the men driven to seek work in the cities, or abroad. Soon the diverted waters of the Euphrates could make this a breadbasket of the Middle East.

Kurdish clan lineages are the oldest family trees on earth – some can be traced back 2500 years. This little group picking cotton belongs to the Beritan tribe, one of the most nomadic. Out of 2000 Beritan families, only 500 have settled. Some have emigrated to the United States, Sweden or Germany, and a fortunate few own hotels or cotton plantations, but the rest have little more than their pride to sustain them.

more personal; for them, Ararat is the symbolic heart of a lost homeland.

No part of the huge social upheaval that went with Turkey's creation was more tragic than the fate of the Armenians, who numbered approximately 2 million in the Ottoman Empire of the early 1900s. They tried to set up their own republic in the bloody confusion of the empire's collapse and at the same time became embroiled as pawns in an international power struggle involving the British, Russians and Turks. Their precise fate is hotly disputed to this day: the Armenians claim that 1.5 million died in massacres and from death-march starvation; Turkey argues that the slaughter was mutual, and that the Armenian losses were much less than that.

Clusters of flat-roofed homes, dominated by the forlorn shell of a Christian church, stand on lonely reaches of the Anatolian highlands, as do grander monuments from earlier times: fortresses, monasteries,

Rural Kurdish women are locked into a patriarchal social code that denies them their rights under Turkish law. Polygamy, although illegal, is still widespread. The prospect of change has been stimulated, however, by the prolonged absences of many husbands as migrant workers in Europe. Left in charge, the women become more confident and self-assertive.

Cotton is a major crop of southern Turkey and an important source of income for many Kurds around Diyarbakir.

The sparseness of the yayla *(mountain pasture) is reflected in the hard life of this semi-nomadic band of Kurds, tied to the constraints and traditions of a vanishing world. At the end of summer, they will fold their tents and descend with the flocks to their village. The film director Yilmaz Guney gained international recognition with* The Herd, *a 1979 drama about such a group threatened by modern development, and the political turmoil that erupts when they decide to take their sheep all the way to Ankara.*

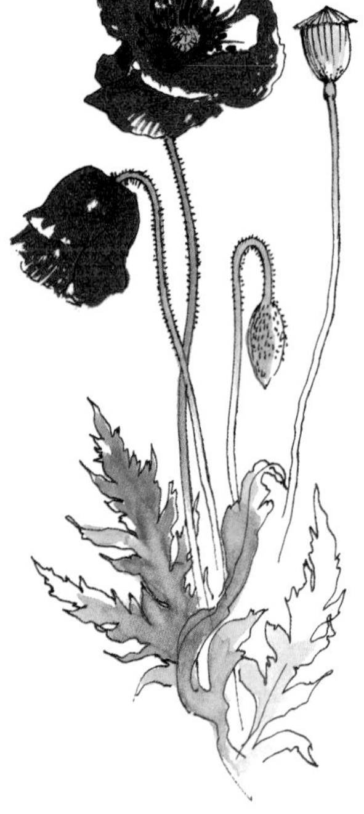

The Anatolian spring is a riotous rebirth that hides the hostile terrain under a dancing carpet of anemones and other wild flowers. When the flowers fade, villagers rely on geraniums planted in tin cans to bring a splash of colour to the tawny landscape of summer.

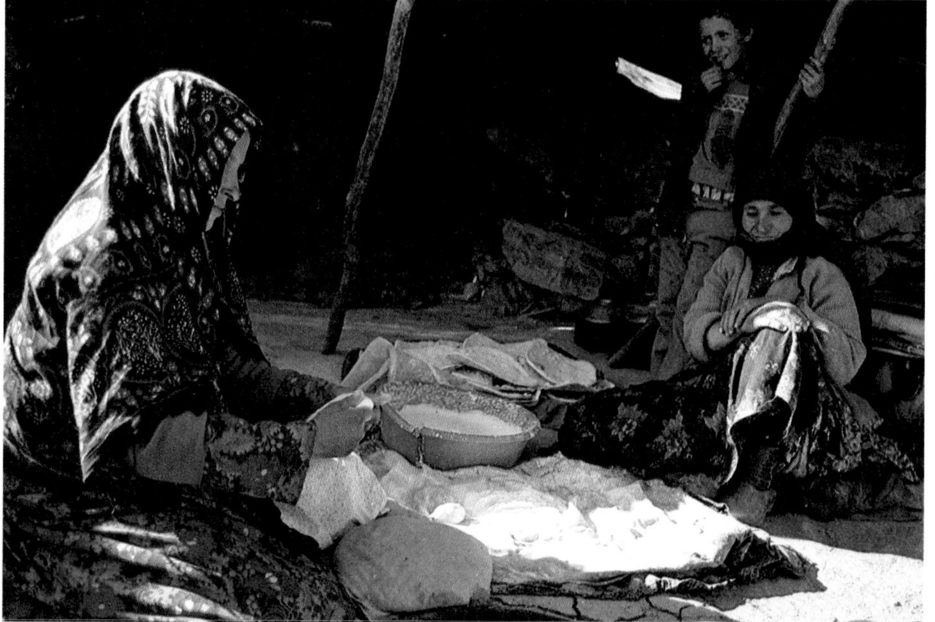

Nomad women prepare yufka *with special care. This wafer-thin flaky pastry is baked on a stone oven and is served stuffed with cheese and herbs. Supplies can be rolled and kept all winter.*

and the great wrecked capital of Ani. The Armenians were master masons, and also claim the distinction of being the very first Christian nation, the conversion of their King Tiridates III taking place a decade ahead of that of the Roman emperor Constantine. By 1980, there were an estimated 60,000 Armenians still living in Turkey, mostly in Istanbul, but with a few tiny, unacknowledged communities still persisting here and there in the highlands.

Brightly garbed women and men with cloth caps and bushy moustaches inhabit many of the old Armenian villages. Former neighbours, these people are Muslim, but no more inclined to be counted as Turks than the previous occupants. They are Kurds, tough mountain pastoralists whose independence can be traced back at least 3000 years. They make up perhaps 80 per cent of the population in eastern Turkey, and perhaps a fifth of the entire Turkish population of 55 million.

Desert miracles

If there was a Kurdish capital, it would be Diyarbakir, a chaotic city of a quarter of a million people that has commanded the southern edge of the plateau for more than 5000 turbulent years. Its awesome Byzantine walls and 72 towers of black basalt loom over the River Tigris, which languidly gathers strength here for its long run to the Persian Gulf. The bustle at a gap punched in the walls is reminiscent of the Galata Bridge: peasants, hawkers, businessmen suited for success, back-packing porters and soldiers, too. In Diyarbakir, the statue of Atatürk requires a 24-hour guard, or so residents like to boast, and the Turkish Seventh Army is on hand to

A woman churns milk into the cheese that forms an important part of the Kurdish diet – as does ayran, *a thirst-quenching drink made of yoghurt whipped up with water and a pinch of salt.*

provide it. The screams of American and Turkish jets from a big airbase are further reminders that the Iraqi border is only 100 miles away.

Beyond Diyarbakir, a desolate wilderness of deep, dry gorge and tired steppe grasps at the headwaters of the Tigris and its twin the Euphrates, parting them before dropping to a hot arid plain. Almost before you realise it, Anatolia has barged into Mesopotamia, and is one with the lands of the Bible. Here, ethnocentric Turkiye must contend with the remains of a score of clashing cultures, where 800 miles of border are shared with an antagonistic Syria, Iraq, and yet more Kurds.

Parallel to the Syrian border – past olive groves and pistachio trees, and sheep and goats wearing blue beads to ward off the evil eye – oil tankers whiz back and forth along a dangerous highway searchlit in places to thwart smugglers and terrorists. A border minefield embraces what remains of Carchemish, the Hittite bastion where Nebuchadnezzar defeated the Egyptian Pharaoh. On bluffs above the desert flats are the snagged remnants of yet another early Christian faith – approximately 30,000 Suriyanis, members of the Syrian Orthodox Church, who speak Aramaic, a tongue dating from the time of Christ, and who have functioning monasteries 1500 years old. Persecuted as heretics by the Crusaders, and then tolerated under Islam, they are now caught in the crossfire of Kurdish unrest. They are celebrated as fine jewellers, but the numbers migrating to Istanbul suggest their slow extinction.

Out on the sun-scorched flats, the plain of Harran is a mirage out of the Old Testament. Here, the Scriptures say, Abraham lived before being directed by God to move on to the land of Canaan. Nearby Urfa has been a holy place since man worshipped the moon and stars; its Cave of Abraham (with separate entrances for men and women) is a Muslim shrine, but its sacred carp have been kept plump in their pools since long before the time of Muhammad, or even of Christ. This is where the contrasts of Turkey reach a climax. Noted for its kebabs and Islamic piety, Urfa is at the epicentre of a boom scheduled to transform the parched badlands of Harran into a breadbasket of the Middle East – and Urfa into the metropolis of eastern Anatolia.

What has filled Urfa's new office blocks with technocrats and brought absentee landlords scurrying back to secure their land claims is a promised miracle of the kind in which Turkish folklore abounds. For Turks, the sound of trickling water has an appeal like no other, and their desert-born religion confers upon fountains a purifying grace. But nothing in faith or fable compares with what has been engineered to the north of Urfa: a complex of a dozen dams (the largest one named, inevitably, after Atatürk) to harness the Euphrates.

The Atatürk Dam is now complete, but it has caused deep controversy. The headwaters of both the Euphrates and Tigris have been affected, and during construction there were – not surprisingly – heated objections from downstream users in Syria and Iraq. It is all a reminder that in the Middle East nothing matters so much as water. It is recorded that even the great Mimar Sinan got into trouble when a fine fountain he designed for himself reduced the supply to the mosque next door.

In Ottoman times Kurdish nomads had no borders to limit their movements. By the late 1960s, there were still about 2 million nomads with large herds of camels and sheep in Turkey, but the government has discouraged the wandering way of life. Those who persevere feel increasingly fenced in, with pastures difficult to find, and a charge levied at every camp site along the way. This little group has halted near Lake Van in the heart of Kurdish territory.

Israel

'If you want it, it need not be a dream' – thus prophesied, in the 1890s, one of the founding fathers of modern Zionism, Theodor Herzl. The dream in question – of founding a State of Israel – had been held by Jewish people for nearly 2000 years, and their faith was to be rewarded. On May 14, 1948, a ceremony in Tel Aviv proclaimed 'the establishment of the Jewish State in Palestine'. At the same time, however, Arab armies were preparing to crush the infant state. What followed is well known: a series of wars, and the running sore of the Palestinian problem. Peace between Jews and Arabs seems ever-elusive, but over 40 years after the state was founded the Israelis are fixed among the world's nations.

The Israeli flag is a half-century older than the country itself: it was first flown in 1897 at the inaugural World Zionist Congress in Basle in Switzerland. The blue bands represent the stripes of the prayer shawl – tallith *– worn by male Jews during worship. The six-pointed star, or shield, of David is an age-old symbol that was first used as an official Jewish emblem 600 years ago in Prague.*

The striped silk coat, wide-brimmed hat, beard and payot *(side whiskers) identify one of the Toldot Aharon – a member of one of several ultra-Orthodox Hassidic sects who congregate in Jerusalem's Mea Shearim district and dress in the styles of 18th-century Poland. Fanatically religious, they question the foundation of the state, since it has pre-empted the coming of the Messiah and does not enforce observance of religious laws.*

Previous page:
Hardy sheep and goats plod the wilderness of Judaea as they have done since the Biblical patriarchs brought their flocks this way 3500-4000 years ago.

The Land of the Bible

They squint as they shuffle into bright sunlight, loaded down with suitcases, boxes and parcels, dogs, cats and small children. Excited, apprehensive, trapped in the 1950s by their tight-fitting suits and shapeless dresses, they arrive by charter aircraft at Ben Gurion Airport. They are what used to be called Soviet Jews. In 1990-91, over a quarter of a million made the *aliya* – 'ascent' – to Israel, and there was talk of the total figure eventually reaching a million.

In the midst of this influx, 15,000 Falashas, the black Jews of Ethiopia, made a confused appearance, plucked from Addis Ababa in a 36-hour airlift codenamed Operation Solomon. Like nationals of a hundred countries before them, these people all arrived by right of the Law of Return which, since the proclamation of the State of Israel on May 14, 1948, has extended to every Jew of the Diaspora (global dispersal) the opportunity of citizenship in a land promised them by their faith. Approximately a quarter of the total world-wide Jewish population of 16 million people is now, by birth or *aliya*, Israeli.

No more than 40 miles to the east of the airport, across the Judaean hills and deep in the valley of the River Jordan, apprehensive travellers of another kind congregate at the crossing point that is Israel's back door to a hostile Arab world. They are Palestinians, some of the one million residents of the West Bank – territories to the west of the Jordan captured by Israel in 1967. (A further 700,000 Palestinians live in the Gaza Strip.) The river that once quickened the pulse of poets is reduced here to a murky trickle; arid gullies and ridges rise on either bank, sheathed in barbed wire and dotted with signs warning 'Danger! Mines!' Emblazoned upon the stark hillside, a large and defiant Star of David faces Jordan. A short distance along the fenced and mined bank is where John is said to have baptised Jesus. Faith and firepower are inextricably mixed here as everywhere else in the Holy Land.

Young Israeli conscripts cradling submachine guns check the transit bus that bumps across the wooden slats of the 100-foot Allenby Bridge, and every Palestinian is liable to a body search for explosives or illicit materials. The process can lead to delays; in the summer of 1992 there were protests when tens of thousands were stalled on the banks of the Jordan amid scenes of chaos and squalor. While permitting freedom of movement, Israel is wary of that other diaspora – the five million Palestinians in nearby countries who hold allegiance to a homeland long ruled by colonial powers and then in 1948 and 1949 reconstituted as Israel and Jordan.

Between bridge and airport, on the stony crest of the Judaean hills, sprawls Jerusalem, sacred to three religions and a large proportion of the world's population, as well as central to the Jewish experience. This is the city revered in both the Old and New Testaments; in Arabic, it is al-Quds, The Holy One. A combination of Benares and Belfast, Jerusalem is arguably the most extraordinary city in the world – 'beyond beliefs', is how an American punster once put it. The 1967 fighting brought all of it under Jewish control for the first time in almost 2000 years, but as Israel's capital it remains a divided salient in this passionately disputed territory. Climb the Mount of Olives for the panorama of rampart and dome, and beyond that of the wilderness stretching out on the far side of the misty, violet Dead Sea to the mountains

The Christian presence in Jerusalem is marked by a complicated and jealous sharing of the holy sites. At least 30 denominations compete for attention, but the older, Eastern churches dominate. This shop selling icons and religious souvenirs in the Old City's Christian Quarter is Greek Orthodox, representing one of the very oldest denominations in Jerusalem.

The narrow streets of Mea Shearim exude the atmosphere of a 19th-century ghetto in Eastern Europe. Puritanical piety reigns here amid the poverty. Families are large. Children as well as adults pray and study the Talmud (books of Jewish law) daily.

OLD YISHUV COURT MUSEUM

where Moses gazed upon the Promised Land . . . and you will not be disappointed. But you will also have to take in some of the less beautiful reality of this uneasy land. Breasting the horizon ahead of you, tall blocks of hastily constructed flats advance in pincer formation, with the Mount of Olives itself topped by a hotel tower. Caught within the grasp, is Arab East Jerusalem still clinging firmly to its separate identity: its own police, school system, business centre, bus network – even its own fire service and electric power grid.

A 50-minute drive from Jerusalem, passing the airport again, and you are in Tel Aviv, the lively beach resort and metropolis that considers itself central to everything in Israeli life other than religion and politics. Within living memory it was little more than sand dunes. Now, close to a third of the Israeli population live or work in its ungainly concrete sprawl, brimming with the street life of many immigrant cultures. About 75 per cent of Israelis live in the long coastal conurbation that has Tel Aviv at its core. The Holy Land is difficult to discern here; if Jerusalem is the City of David, then Tel Aviv is the city of the McDavid cheeseburger, and when Jerusalem shuts down for the Sabbath, Tel Aviv lets its hair down for the weekend. When Iraqi Scud missiles began landing here in 1991, it was a sobering reminder to the residents of Tel Aviv that their enemies are never more than a bus ride away.

The grand illusion

For all its military victories (five wars won in 40 years, rivalling anything in the Old Testament), Israel remains a small country, a stretched-out Wales – 260 miles long by 70 miles at its widest – if one can imagine a Wales that is more than 50 per cent desert. Shaped like a rough hewn flint from one of its own innumerable prehistoric sites, Israel is wedged between sea and desert, its inside edge dug into the deepest trench on the face of the earth: the Jordan Rift. The result is an incredible diversity of climate and landscape, and a consequent illusion of size.

Tourist brochures like to stress how it is possible – in times of peace, at least – to take an early morning ski run down the slopes of Mount Hermon on the border with Lebanon in the far north and then to drive down to the country's southernmost tip in time for an evening of scuba-diving among the coral reefs and tropical fish of the Red Sea at Elat. Sights along the way would include the Negev Desert and the eerie Dead Sea, at 1300 feet below sea level the lowest point on the earth's surface. Far swifter and almost as varied is the short ride from Jerusalem to Jericho – a route made famous in the parable of the Good Samaritan. Amos Elon, writing about Jerusalem, recommends waiting for a snowy winter's day, and making the point of departure the ultramodern campus of the Hebrew University on Mount Scopus. The ride down takes 20 minutes, and transports the traveller from a frigid, futuristic world of satellite dishes to a Bedouin encampment basking under palm trees, interspersed with banana groves and blossoming flame trees, in the eternal summer of the famous Biblical oasis.

At 820 feet below sea level, Jericho is the lowest and possibly the oldest walled town in the world; this is the place to acquire a new historical perspective. The mudbrick walls excavated from the *tel* (mound) of the

Highly egalitarian and highly visible, the Israeli army is like no other. Basic training extends to courses in history, making this museum in the reconstructed Jewish Quarter of the Old City an object for study as well as for protection.

The Dome of the Rock is a poignant symbol of the conflict between Islam and Israel. The oldest of all Muslim shrines, it stands on the site of the temples of Solomon and Herod. Orthodox Jews either consider the area too holy to approach, or have intemperate visions of building a third Temple here.

The ancient port of Jaffa has been swallowed up – rather like Jonah who sailed from here to his encounter with the whale. Although now part of bustlingly modern Tel Aviv, Jaffa retains something of the atmosphere of the old Middle East. Its name means 'beautiful' in Hebrew, but it might just possibly derive from Japheth, *the name of Noah's son and its reputed founder.*

A small boy sets out on a quest for religious enlightenment that could last his lifetime. Judaism is a complex faith with a vast accumulation of sacred literature. The basis of belief is the Torah which consists of the five books of Moses and contains 613 commandments of God. This is supplemented by the prophetic and other books of the Old Testament. The Talmud, meanwhile, amounts to 63 books of rabbinical interpretations of the scriptures and of commentaries touching upon all the various aspects of life. More than 50,000 students currently attend yeshivot *(religious schools) in Israel, in an extraordinary resurgence of interest in Orthodox Judaism.*

ancient city, while not too dissimilar from the walls of the nearby Palestinian refugee camp, are pre-Biblical, and therefore not the ones that are said to have collapsed before the trumpets of Joshua. Jericho was more than 7000 years old when the Israelites reached the Promised Land, and Joshua's assault was comparatively of such recent date that any evidence of it has been washed away with erosion of the topsoil.

Ready for Armageddon

From Jericho the road slices through Samaria, as Israel terms the bulge of occupied West Bank territory to the north of Jerusalem (the occupied zone to the south of the city has reverted to its Biblical name of Judaea). The stony landscape becomes picture-book Middle East: olive groves rustling in the hot wind, old men riding tiny donkeys, women with burdens on their heads. There is a less benign note: the hills are dotted with watchtowers and antennae, and the army is widely present. This does not deter Palestinian youths from stoning vehicles with Israeli licence plates, however. They are daring the wrath of well-armed Jewish settlers drawn here by a religious compulsion to reclaim Biblical lands, and formerly, often by generous government financial incentives as well. The neat white blocks of Jewish settlements (largely constructed with Arab labour) form a well-planned strategic network, commanding the high ground over the Arab towns and villages, linked by radio to one another and the army posts.

Samaria tumbles on to the broad and lush Jezreel Valley. According to the Book of Revelations, this is where the forces of good and evil will fight history's final Battle of Armageddon; if so, Israeli warplanes are ready, swooping low over a big airbase. Across the valley lie Nazareth and the hills of Galilee, cradle of Christianity, and cause for another miraculous mood-swing. Here, just an hour's drive away from the epicentre of Middle East tensions, busloads of Christian pilgrims gaze in wonder over the waters of the little 'Sea' of Galilee – now known as Lake Tiberias (or Yam Kinneret in Hebrew), and measuring just 13 miles by seven. This is where Jesus walked, and where he gathered together the disciples Simon and Andrew, James and John, and the others (including his betrayer Judas Iscariot). At the town of Tiberias, new hotels tower over a shoreline of outdoor restaurants serving the lake's distinctive St Peter's fish. The air is soft and warm, the water satin, and upon it a ferryboat glides towards the kibbutz of Ein Gev, trailing laughter and pop music.

As night falls upon the lake, a string of lights twinkles reassurance from settlements on the

Israeli markets can match any around the Mediterranean, with a diversity of produce to meet a uniquely diverse demand. Israel has yet to develop a single cuisine of its own, and makes do with a hotch-potch of immigrant culinary traditions with little in common except a general adherence to the basic kosher rules, such as separating meat and milk products. The favourite snack is not even Jewish in origin: the ubiquitous felafel *– chickpea fritters, crispy salad and* tehina *or sesame sauce stuffed into a pitta bread pouch.*

A soft-drink seller with traditional dispenser lends colour to the Muslim Quarter of the Old City in Jerusalem. Sharp cultural divisions between the walled city's four quarters – Muslim, Christian, Armenian, and Jewish – date back for centuries.

escarpment of the Golan Heights, a strategic plateau to the north-east captured from Syria in 1967, lost and recaptured in an epic 1973 tank battle, and still encrusted with all the trappings of a war zone – deserted shell-pocked villages, rusting battle debris, army camps and tank parks, and Israeli and Syrian lookouts training binoculars on one another, with a fragile United Nations peacekeeping force squeezed in between. But it is Israel that today commands the high ground, with Damascus down the gun barrel. And amid tank traps and minefields at the very edge of no-man's-land grow the vines that produce Israel's best wine – wine so kosher that only Orthodox Jews (and no women) may have a hand in its production.

Looking for Moses

Location partly explains the impact of this meagre strip of land upon the world. This was the narrow corridor of communication between the great civilisations of the ancient Middle East – between Egypt and Babylon: the Way of the Sea, as it was called in Roman times. Armies and ideas had banged back and forth for thousands of years before the concept of one unseen god for all mankind arose. How it happened, only the Bible will claim to say with confidence, but archaeology is digging deeper and deeper into the crevices between fact, myth and faith. Abraham's nomadic odyssey is dated at around 1800 BC – about the time when ancient Britons were putting the finishing touches to Stonehenge – and that of Moses a few hundred years later. There is little certain archaeological evidence of these Biblical super-heroes, or of Joshua or David or Isaiah, but the accuracy of incidental details in the Old Testament is regularly confirmed by the diggers.

Very occasionally, a voice emerges from out of the distant past. It happened in the case of a series of dispatches from one Abdu-Heba, an embattled vassal king of 'Urusalim' found in the archives of the Egyptian Pharaoh Amenhotep III, dating from around 1400 BC, or about the time when Moses is now reckoned to have lived. 'Send archers . . . send troops of archers,' the king pleads, with increasing desperation. He sends the Pharaoh a gift of 21 maidens, but still no help arrives, not even when he reports that Bethlehem – only five miles from Jerusalem – has gone over to the enemy. The dispatches cease abruptly, the outcome unrecorded, but the invading host are identified as 'the Habiru', and it is tempting to speculate that this might have been an advance force of the Hebrews, otherwise known as the Children of Israel, and later called the Jews, after the Biblical kingdom of Judah.

Archaeology is politics in Israel, and a national obsession whose effects are evident nowhere more than in Jerusalem. Centuries of debris have been carted away to lay bare blackened evidence of the sacking by Nebuchadnezzar in 586 BC, as well as charred homes

The donkey is as familiar a sight in the Holy Land today as it was when it carried the holy family on the flight into Egypt 2000 years ago.

and bones from the terrible destruction wrought in AD 70 at the command of the Roman Emperor Titus. The Jewish quarter of the Old City has also been reconstructed with a wide square before the Western ('Wailing') Wall. This is a massive remnant of the containing wall of the Temple Mount, the huge platform on which the temples of Solomon and Herod once stood, and where Jews for centuries have lamented their loss and prayed for messianic deliverance.

The Temple Mount itself stays inviolate, at least for now. This is ground zero in the confrontation between Israeli and Arab, Jew and Muslim. This spot was the Holy of Holies where the ancient Jews worshipped their unseen God. But Muslims too have been worshipping their God in this place for 1300 years, barring occasional interludes, especially that between 1099 and 1187 when Christian Crusaders captured Jerusalem and put off-limits what can only be described as a foundation stone of monotheism. The stone is a rock slab, roughly 50 feet by 60 feet, protruding from the ground and since AD 691 enshrined within the lustrous, peacock-hued Mosque of Omar, or Dome of the Rock. According to Muslim tradition, this is the spot from which Muhammad sprang to heaven on his horse. It is also the sacred rock upon which King David built the altar of the Lord, and is regarded as the site of Abraham's near-sacrifice of his son Isaac, not to mention Cain's murder of Abel and – in the fullness of time – the Last Judgement.

To complete the eternal triangle of creeds focused upon the One Godhead, the cupola of the Church of the Holy Sepulchre rises above the flat rooftops, a few minutes' walk from the Dome of the Muslims and the Wall of the Jews; here the places regarded as the sites of the Crucifixion, burial and Resurrection of Christ are contained within a single cluttered set of premises

This elderly Palestinian of Hebron in the Israeli-occupied West Bank is witness to tense confrontations between Jewish settlers and local Muslims over a Biblical city that is sacred to both. The focus of emotion is the reputed tomb of the patriarchs Abraham, Isaac and Jacob. Israeli troops maintain an uneasy peace.

Jerusalem's old walled city has been a key tourist attraction since its capture from Jordan in the Six Day War of June 1967. But tourist numbers dwindled under the impact of the intifada *revolt against Israeli authority, when strikes and violent incidents became commonplace.*

(Calvary upstairs, tomb in the basement), rancorously shared among half a dozen of Jerusalem's 30 or more Christian sects.

David Street is where they converge and divide – Christians swinging left to the Holy Sepulchre, Jews branching off right to the Western Wall, Muslims continuing straight on to the mosques on the Temple Mount. The street is a packed bazaar loaded with olive wood crucifixes and Stars of David, spices and Bedouin daggers, and T-shirts declaring 'I Got Stoned on the West Bank'. Church bells boom, clang, chime and peal, while from the minarets the muezzins' taped calls reverberate around the alleyways, the amplifiers turned up during times of tension. Pious Jews seem not to notice as they sway back and forth before the Wall, oblivious also to the army helicopter whirring overhead, the camera-clicking tourists, and the *bar mitzvah* party from New York chanting '*mazeltov, mazeltov*' as their 13-year-old boy is carried shoulder high around the square as part of the ceremony that confers on him the privileges and responsibilities of Jewish male adulthood. On top of the wall soldiers stand alert, guns slung at the ready, as always.

Chatting with the prophets

What would the patriarchs and the prophets, the disciples and the apostles, make of it all? They would have no trouble with the currency, though they might need to be warned about Israel's notorious inflation (50 shekels no longer buys the Temple Mount, as it did in King David's day – it buys, in 1993, an electric kettle perhaps). The disciples would have to learn Hebrew, for this was no longer the mother tongue in Christ's day. The people of the New Testament spoke mainly Aramaic, the lingua franca of much of the Middle East in those days (and still spoken in parts of Syria, Lebanon and Turkey): it took 19th-century Zionist ingenuity to restore Hebrew to everyday life from the scrolls of the sacred Torah. So Prime Minister Yitzhak Rabin could chat with Moses, and give the Old Testament patriarch a rough-and-ready sense of late 20th-century politics; Rabin might also try mentioning that *Palestinian* is a Romanised form of *Philistine,* the name for that doughty Biblical foe of the Israelites, fought and cursed from Genesis to Zechariah, from Delilah to Goliath.

The prophet Ezekiel, meanwhile, might be pleasurably surprised by various other things he found in contemporary Israel. The Biblical promise of 'a land flowing with milk and honey' was never quite the soft option it might have seemed. Bible 'honey' was the mashed fruit of the date palm, scholars say, and goats would have supplied most of the milk in this rugged, thirsty land that stumbled into the desolation of the Negev below Beersheba. But read Ezekiel and you will find him foretelling a day when a river would traverse the desert and that 'everything shall live whither the river cometh'. Ezekiel was right, though he surely did not have in mind that the river would be the Jordan. It is tapped upstream in the natural reservoir of Lake

Though a variety of citrus fruits are marketed under the 'Jaffa' label, it is the Jaffa orange that has come to symbolise Israel in supermarkets around the world. More than 150 years ago, the French statesman-poet Alphonse de Lamartine described the port of Jaffa as 'surrounded by delectable gardens . . . full of white orange blossom'.

'The experiment that worked' was philosopher Martin Buber's description of the institution that defined pioneer Israel in the eyes of the world – the agricultural commune known as the kibbutz. Having made the desert bloom, the kibbutz system meets half Israel's food needs and for many years provided the backbone of the country's political and military leadership.

Tiberias, and in a spectacular feat of plumbing – prosaically named the National Water Carrier – its water is piped 80 miles across the hills of Galilee, down the coastal plain, and into the Negev south-west of Beersheba. In a world of expanding deserts, the Israeli wilderness continues to retreat before the advance of cotton fields and orange groves.

The kibbutzniks

'We shall keep our rabbis within their synagogues, just as we shall keep our armies inside their barracks', vowed Theodor Herzl, the 19th-century visionary of Zionism, the movement that fostered the birth of Israel. Herzl wanted nothing to do with Jerusalem, rating it

The farmer-warrior ready at a moment's notice to leap from his tractor to the controls of a tank is a key figure in modern Israeli mythology. However, agriculture is no longer as important as it used to be. More than 80 per cent of Israelis are now city dwellers.

Taming the desert is the task of scientists at world-renowned research institutes attached to Ben Gurion University in the Negev capital, Beersheba. A tomato that thrives on salt water and a prickly pear without prickles are typical accomplishments. Some research has a political side-effect. By studying ways to help poor and parched countries improve their lot, Israel earns international good will.

irredeemably sunk in 'superstition and fanaticism'. Rather, he fancied a new start with a new capital, built on high ground overlooking the Mediterranean. As it turned out, the visionary was no prophet, yet the egalitarian ideals of the early Zionists endure in two of Israel's most vaunted institutions, the kibbutz and the Zahal, or military forces.

The concept of the kibbutz (Hebrew for 'a grouping') went to the heart of the Zionist dream of creating a utopian society rooted in the ancestral soil. It also drew some inspiration from Karl Marx and the early, idealistic Russian revolutionaries. Kibbutzim are agricultural settlements in which everything is owned and shared collectively – 'from each according to his abilities, to each according to his needs'. The first experimental kibbutz was established by a handful of settlers on the banks of the Jordan in the region of Galilee in 1909, well before the State of Israel was formed. By the 1920s, there were more than a score of

The Galilean hill country of dusty olive groves and braying donkeys abounds in scenes like this. Allowing for minor discrepancies such as a plastic bag, they can barely have changed since the boyhood of Jesus.

The Galilean village of Kafr Kanna, a few miles outside Nazareth, is the purported site of Christ's first miracle, when he changed water into wine at the wedding feast. Some scholars suspect that an unexcavated site in the hills to the east of here is, in fact, the Biblical Cana, but such quibbling has little impact on a tradition, going back at least 1700 years, that places Cana at Kafr Kanna. Many other holy places of uncertain authenticity have been similarly sanctified by ages of acceptance.

communities, reclaiming wasteland, draining swamps, and coincidentally beginning to form a security cordon around the expanding Jewish immigrant community. In the 1990s, they number more than 270, and are to be found everywhere from mountain top to desert. Size varies, but most consist of a few hundred members who are supposed to have no private wealth, and no need of any, since their welfare is assured from cradle to grave. Their success can be judged from the fact that the great majority of kibbutzim have now reached their third generation, at least. The movement also has its own education system and cultural and business support networks.

Kibbutzniks are an élite. They account for little more than 3 per cent of the Israeli population, but they supply the country with half its food needs and exert an

influence that is similarly out of proportion to their numbers. Three of Israel's first six prime ministers were kibbutzniks, as were a third of all cabinet ministers in the early decades of nationhood. The pattern holds in combat as well: kibbutzim contributed a third of the pilots who fought in the Six Day War of 1967, and sustained almost the same proportion of fatal casualties in that war. Yet times are changing. The rise of the political right in Israel has diminished the kibbutzim's influence, while affluence has had a profoundly mellowing effect. A typical kibbutz today has the appearance more of a country club than of a pioneer outpost. Many employ Arab labour in their fields, and almost all have branched into industry, with hopes increasingly pinned on high technology enterprises. Just how much has changed became clear when the late Menachem Begin (the non-kibbutznik Prime Minister from 1977 to 1983) was able to score political points by

mocking 'those kibbutzniks and their swimming pools'!

In the 'heroic' age, the khaki-clad kibbutzniks shared even their underwear; privacy, like private property, was taboo, and the most radical communities tended to regard marriage as bourgeois backsliding. Such attitudes have largely vanished, to the point where communal raising of children has been widely abandoned. The stridently irreligious tone that characterised their earlier years has also been tempered, and there are now a number of religious kibbutzim. And while the mainstream shuns synagogues and stays resolutely socialist and agnostic, Jewish cultural roots are still nourished; so, for example, at dinner on Friday night, the traditional plaited *challah* bread makes its appearance, and the communal dining room is decked with tablecloths, candles and the traditional small cups of wine.

The ever-ready army

Egalitarian kibbutz values have filtered throughout Israeli society, nowhere more than in the Israeli Defence Force, which developed out of the Palmach, the kibbutzim militia of the days before the Israeli State was formed. Nonchalant, irreverent, outspoken, the Israeli soldier is like no other. He, or she, is a universal presence . . . strolling the streets, lounging in cafés, checking bags and parcels at the entrance to supermarkets, hitching lifts at every road junction. 'Would you mind moving your gun, please?' is a familiar request in the ever-crowded buses. In a nation born out of war, and in a state of at least nominal war ever since, military service is mandatory for all Israelis, except the Arab minority, members of which can, however, volunteer to serve. Ultra-Orthodox Jews are

This timeless scene comes from the so-called Arab Triangle of farming villages on the coastal plain east of Tel Aviv. It obscures growing prosperity, on the one hand, and restiveness, on the other, among Arab Israelis who complain that they are denied full equality as loyal citizens.

A casualty of peace – this snack bar on the Red Sea coast south of Elat has seen a drastic drop in customers since Israel returned Sinai to Egypt following the 1978 Camp David Agreement. None the less, Israelis prepared to put up with visa and other tedious border formalities are still welcome to explore the great desert and climb the mountain traditionally identified as the one where Moses received the Ten Commandments.

No more than 10 per cent of Israel's 70,000 Bedouin still lead a semi-nomadic life on the fringe of the Negev, and the days are gone when they could roam freely with their flocks. Displaced by the advance of Jewish agricultural settlements and the requisition of huge tracts of the Negev for military manoeuvres, firing ranges and airfields, many have been obliged to find labouring jobs in urban settlements. Hope for the future lies in education, which the Bedouin take seriously.

permitted to delay their call-up until their religious studies have been completed. Call-up age is 18. Women serve two years, men serve three – four in the case of the air force and navy – and then they serve at least a month of reserve duty each year until they are well into their fifties.

Some aspects of militarism are eschewed. Saluting is perfunctory; uniforms are not always uniform, and officers and other ranks are generally on first-name terms, eating the same food in the same mess. The military code states that an officer has no privileges, only duties; it is a point of pride that there is no command 'Forward' in the Israeli army, only 'Follow me'. The effect is that of an extended family rather than a war machine, with each casualty being of personal concern to all.

'The secret of this country,' a doctor from Haifa in the north once suggested, 'is that there is no unknown soldier.' Less high-flown is the anecdote about the two soldiers who are blocking the pavement, deep in conversation, when a general edges past. The soldiers keep talking, hands in pockets. The general doubles back, and addresses one of the soldiers, 'Well, Yoram, are you angry?'

'No, why?'

'You didn't say hello!'

The Bedouin of the Negev are split into more than 20 tribal groupings. Even the most traditional are quick to take advantage of the modern world. This mother almost certainly had her baby in Beersheba Hospital.

The desert dwellers of the Negev are not considered a security threat. Bedouins are recruited into the Israeli forces as scouts and trackers, and a few have reached senior rank. The Druse are another Arab minority group trusted by the Israelis. About as numerous as the Bedouin, they serve in the military and have a reputation for bravery.

Stirring the pot

With a single platoon liable to include immigrants from a dozen countries, the army is the spoon that stirs the Israeli melting pot, throwing together almost every ethnic, national, and social group. As soon as the state was secured in 1948, the army's role as 'the cultural instrument for assimilation' was encouraged by Prime Minister David Ben Gurion, and ever since 1949 it has had an educational role as well, teaching immigrant conscripts the Hebrew language, Israeli history and other basics: how many other armies run nature study courses? The Israeli Defence Force has even managed to develop a standardised synagogue acceptable to all branches of Judaism, and regulations that are tolerable to all, including the Orthodox warrior. Thus, leave is arranged so that no soldier need travel on the Sabbath, and there is an exemption from sounding the ceremonial *shofar* (ram's horn) near enemy lines when that would give away the Israeli position.

Shared military experience is helping to dissipate the cultural clash between Jews of European origin and the Oriental Jews mainly from Arab lands – including large 'ingatherings' of Moroccan, Iraqi and Yemeni Jews – who in the 1960s were in danger of becoming an underclass. By the 1980s, the tables were turned: the Oriental Jews, with larger families, had achieved a clear numerical advantage that translated into political clout. With a quarter of Israeli marriages mixed, it was the turn of the European Jews to fret now – about what was termed Levantinism, or the gradual Middle Easternising of the country at the expense of the Western cultural values of its founders.

Jackets off and sleeves rolled up, these Orthodox Jews are performing morning prayers with the obligatory use of tefillin *– small black leather boxes containing sacred texts on parchment that are strapped to head and arm. The tradition is that this will ensure that God's commands influence the thoughts (through the head) and deeds (through the arm) of the wearer. The practice has also been described as 'plugging in to the divine mains'.*

The consequence, thus far, is an amazing mingle. Take Dimona, the Negev Desert site of Israel's top-secret nuclear research plant. Dimona boasts a cricket team manned by Jews who came to Israel from India, a maverick community of black Americans who claim to be the 'real Jews', and a classical music conservatory staffed by Jews of Russian extraction catering to a population that mostly came from Morocco and with no previous exposure to the world of Mozart and Beethoven. (Dimona also, fairly typically, has an unemployment problem.) Music is a good example of the exotic cross-fertilisations taking place. While Israel has a higher percentage of classical concertgoers than any other country, the young are increasingly tuning to home-brewed Hebrew pop that melds Western with Arabic rhythms.

Sabra is the popular term for a native-born Israeli – named after the prickly pear, the fruit with a spiky exterior but a surprisingly sweet, soft inside. Sabras now account for more than half the population. They are a dynamic new Jewish prototype, forthright and individualistic to the point of often appearing arrogant. 'Israelis have no manners. None', was the flat conclusion of Stephen Brook, the English (and Jewish) travel writer. 'We're impatient because we're nervous', an English-Israeli anthropologist told Brook. 'We're insecure, so we appear arrogant.' Living with danger, Israelis seem to invite it, as when crowds flock around a bomb-disposal expert examining a suspect package. They drive the badly maintained roads with such fury (500 road deaths in this small country each year) that air conditioning is standard equipment in new cars as a contribution towards cooling emotions.

Pick any two Israelis, the saying goes, and you have three opinions, loudly expressed. Through the nation's short, violent existence, the external threat has assured unity, but some have speculated that an Israel at peace would tear itself apart. Israel has no constitution, only an unresolved contradiction between its status as the Jewish state and its aspiration to be a secular democracy with equal rights for citizens of all creeds. Even the most basic of issues – Who is a Jew? – is a subject of continuing and bitter dispute between rival factions.

Zionism was a heresy to pious believers who held that the rebirth of the Jewish nation must await the coming of the Messiah. Through the ages, little communities had kept vigil in the Holy Land, waiting expectantly for his arrival. And some still do, in ultra-Orthodox redoubts such as Mea Shearim in Jerusalem, and in Safed, on a Galilean hillside, where the chants of hundreds of black-clad Hassidim – members of a mystical sect founded originally in Poland around 1750 – echo through the cobbled streets each Friday at sunset.

Orthodox Judaism and its set of laws and customs – known as the *halacha* – evolved largely in the Diaspora, and Zionists expected it to dwindle into insignificance with the achievement of nationhood. But it has not, and Jerusalem is filled with *yeshivot*, religious schools, both for undeviatingly pious students and for born-again Jews wishing to return to the Orthodox fold. More portentous was the emergence, in the wake of Israel's martial triumphs, of a brand of militant Jewish fundamentalism combining Orthodoxy with nationalism, and exemplified by the young zealot in T-shirt and jeans, wearing *kippa* skullcap on his head and holstered pistol in his belt.

Most Israeli Jews are not deeply religious, and many who follow a kosher diet, celebrate religious holidays, and have their sons circumcised do so for a mixture of historical, religious and cultural reasons rather than for religious reasons alone. But the ultra-Orthodox minority wields enormous, and disproportionate, power in national affairs by virtue of the leverage that the small religious parties are able to exert in the Knesset (parliament) under Israel's elaborate system of proportional representation. By this means both Reform and Conservative Judaism, which developed in the West as ways of adapting the religion to modern life, have been consistently denied official recognition. The power of the Orthodox can be seen in other ways, too. There is no civil marriage or divorce in Israel, for example, and no facilities for Jew to marry non-Jew: the only way around the law is to marry abroad, commonly in nearby Cyprus.

The most important meal of the week in Jewish homes is dinner on Friday night at the start of Shabbat *– the Sabbath. The house has been cleaned and the family's best crockery and linen laid out. Orthodox fathers take their sons to the synagogue while the women prepare the meal, which is meticulously kosher* (kasher, *'proper' in Hebrew) – prepared in accordance with minutely detailed dietary laws derived from the Old Testament. Among Orthodox Jews, no work of any kind may be undertaken until* Shabbat *ends on Saturday evening.*

The Western ('Wailing') Wall, a massive fragment of the retaining wall of the Temple destroyed by the Romans in AD 70, was the supreme prize of the 1967 war that re-united the whole of Jerusalem under Jewish rule for the first time in almost 2000 years. The focal point of the Jewish world, it is attended round the clock by an endless stream of worshippers, pilgrims and tourists.

Pious policing of the Sabbath – from Friday sunset to Saturday evening – is another contentious issue. Except in the more secular areas of the country, public transport, restaurants and places of entertainment all shut down, while hotels adjust their weekday routines, such as by setting lifts to run an automatic floor-by-floor shuttle. This gets round the traditional injunction against lighting a fire on the Sabbath – nowadays also applied to switching on an electric current.

The forgotten Israelis

'I am an Arab, a Palestinian, a Christian, and a citizen of the State of Israel', Canon Riah Abu el-Assal, head of the Anglican Church in Nazareth, told the BBC's Gerald Butt. 'Little wonder that outsiders get confused.' One in every six Israelis is Arab – three-quarters of a million descendants and remnants of that part of the Arab population of Mandate Palestine which did not flee the violence and chaos of the war that accompanied Israel's birth in 1948. Concentrated mainly in Galilee, with pockets in Jaffa, Haifa and Acre, they carry Israeli passports and vote in Israeli elections – and a handful sit in the Knesset – but they are a people kept apart, exempt from military service and excluded from certain jobs and state benefits. Social mixing between Jews and Arabs is minimal; intermarriage is extremely rare.

The Anglican Canon points to the diversity of Israeli Arabs: most are Muslim, but Christians are a significant minority; then there are the Druse, a mountain people who broke from Islam 900 years ago and observe their own secret rites, while the tent-dwelling Bedouin are another, scattered group living in every sense on the fringe. For exclusivity, however, there is nothing to compare with the Samaritans: dwindled to less than 600 at the last count, they have their own holy mountain and claim to be the world's smallest ethnic group and the true spiritual heirs of the Tribes of Israel.

The strain on Arab Israelis intensified after December 9, 1987, when their kith and kin under military rule in the occupied territories launched the *intifada*, a mismatched war of youths flinging stones and petrol bombs against the might of the Israeli army, but effective in drawing the world's attention to their plight. By literally taking up the sling of a David, these youths turned Israel into an ugly Goliath on the world's television screens: the heroic victor of wars of survival now found itself trapped in the unsavoury role of a sometimes brutal occupying force. 'My country is at war with my people', became the constantly expressed lament in Galilee and other Arab strongholds. The nation which had started out with such high hopes just under 40 years earlier had yet to resolve some of the harsher and more intractable realities of its existence.

An Israeli without a military record carries a stigma. Women too are called up for national service at the age of 18, and though no longer sent into combat – as happened in 1948 – they are trained as instructors. It is not uncommon to see female sergeants drilling platoons of male reserves, many of whom are old enough to be their fathers, or teaching conscripts how to fire machine guns or drive tanks.

Saudi Arabia

As early as the 10th century BC, the camel trains of King Solomon were penetrating the sandy wastes of Arabia in search of incense and spices to be found beyond them. In this landscape of desert extremes, the sacred and the secular have always been closely intertwined for the wandering tribes of the Bedouin. And Arabia was always a meeting place of ideas as well as goods: it was here, after all, in the 7th century AD that the new religion of Islam was born. Nowadays, the state of Saudi Arabia – founded in 1932 by King Abdul Aziz ibn Saud – is a place of fabulous wealth, the largest oil-producing nation in the world, but it still clings fast to strict Muslim beliefs and ways.

Weaving is basic to Bedouin life, for it is on the distinctively long, narrow loom that the women create the cloth strips that make up the family tent. The tent interior is enlivened with brightly coloured dividing curtains, rugs, bags and camel trappings, all made on the same loom.

Every Saudi is at heart a Bedouin, and the city dweller sometimes feels a compelling need to drive into the desert to experience the sensation of supreme solitude that is central to his ancestral experience.

Previous page:
The level gaze and fine-drawn features stamp him as true Bedouin. He has abandoned herding camels for sheep, which he carries by lorry from sparse pasture to pasture. But no matter how much he and his kind have been obliged to adapt, they remain a powerful prototype that influences Saudi Arabian attitudes and values.

The Land of Black Gold

In January 1902, a Bedouin raiding party emerged from the mysterious Rub al Khali (Empty Quarter) of the Arabian desert and stole by night into the oasis of Riyadh, killing the sheikh in a dawn melee and capturing the mud-walled fort. Riyadh was too remote to be accurately pinpointed on any map, and the raid seemed like many another in the warring rhythm of desert life. But the victor, a rival sheikh's son named Abdul Aziz ibn Abdul Rahman ibn Saud, did not stop with the recapture of the citadel from which his father had been driven a dozen years before. He fought on, until he ruled a wilderness the size of Western Europe, upon which, in 1932, he bestowed his family name, and under which oil was shortly discovered – more oil than anywhere else on earth.

Abdul Aziz ibn Saud, creator and first king of Saudi Arabia – Arabia of the al-Saud – died in 1953, a patriarch of biblical stature. He sired 43 sons, some of whom proved equally potent, so that the House of Saud now has several thousand princes, to say nothing of princesses. It is by far the largest, richest, and most powerful dynasty on earth.

And their kingdom has changed in proportion. Dune buggies now cavort where early European travellers used to sweat. Motorways slash across the wastes, turning ancient camel caravan routes into asphalt strips. The dwindling ranks of Bedouin who persist in the nomadic life stow their black tents and their wives and children in the back of little four-wheel-drive Japanese trucks, and carry water to their herds by diesel tanker. Riyadh is very much on the map. It entered the 1990s with one of the highest urban growth rates in the world, concreting over the desert at the rate of several square miles per year.

But just as the mud fort has survived Riyadh's stunning transformation – with the tip of a lance flung by Abdul Aziz's raiders still embedded in its heavy wooden door – so traditional desert values, harking back to the time of the prophet Abraham, have remained.

The desert kingdom

Arabia is effectively an enormous desert island, cut off from the rest of the Middle East by a barrier of sand dunes known as the Nafud, and by expanses of hard-packed grit and rock that look like the pictures the Voyager spacecraft sent back from Mars. Here was the marshalling area for Operation Desert Storm – a landscape 'so awful in its perfect flatness I thought I could see the curvature of the earth,' wrote one Western war correspondent.

The Arabian interior is further sealed by mountains. The high, jagged peaks of the Hejaz on the west dovetail into a bare brown southern escarpment, like castle walls before the Red and Arabian seas. Within these walls, the Empty Quarter occupies a quarter of a million square miles, the largest body of continuous sand in the world. Even the Bedouin have traditionally avoided its hostile wastes; the first European to cross it was the British writer Bertram Thomas in 1930 who used the one well-watered route. Other adventurers (including another British traveller, Wilfred Thesiger) have followed where Thomas led, but to this day much of the Empty Quarter remains as empty as ever and unexplored. Between the sands of the Empty Quarter and the sands of the Nafud, meanwhile, lies the Najd, an arid, rough wilderness dusted with wandering dunes known as *barchands* and sprinkled with fertile oases; this is the heartland of Arabia.

The sun in summer blazes like a blowtorch. The

Camels make up the dairy herds of the desert. Bull camels are usually killed for meat when young, now that they are not needed as pack animals.

temperature can top 50°C (122°F) in the shade – where there is shade. In winter, it can dip to 0°C (32°F). Rainfall is sparse and irregular; a few inches per annum at best, sometimes nothing for years. Plant life has nevertheless adapted – stunted tamarisk, acacia and prickly saltbushes that can survive on almost nothing – and it takes only a splash of spring rain for grass dotted with tiny bright flowers to sprout amid the desolation. The summer capital Taif in the mountains above Mecca is famous for its roses and pomegranates, and the Asir mountains of the south open up a different world altogether: wild flowers clothe their slopes in spring and large areas of them are covered with dense forests. Leopards, cheetahs, jackals, and their prey, gazelles and various small mammals, manage to survive in various parts of the country. Baboons are found in the mountains; sand cats, honey badgers and *hyrakes* (the 'coney' referred to in the Bible) live in the desert. Migrant birds from Europe rest along the Red Sea coast, and falcons are highly prized and trained for hunting. Snakes and scorpions thrive, and so does the camel. The rich underwater life of the Red Sea has been made famous by the French film-maker Jacques Cousteau.

The camel – domesticated around 2500 BC – was man's way into the desert. There man planted date-palm seeds in gulleys and wadis where ground water seeped near the surface to give succulence, shade and grace to the oases. 'The date is the mother and the aunt of the Arabs', or so the saying goes. The word Arab is thought to derive from abhar, a Semitic word meaning to move or pass (the word Hebrew is thought to come from the same root), but the meaning broadened as people settled, and the Arabic word for a nomad is badawi – hence the Bedu, or Bedouin.

Arabs despise dogs as unclean, but the sleek Saluki hunting dog is an exception. The Bedouin prize and pamper this handsome relative of the greyhound.

'We are the Bedu . . .'

The boundless horizons gave a sense of liberty, but the hostile environment presented harsh terms for survival. The family was the unit of existence; survival alone was impossible. Families bonded tightly into extended families, or clans, sharing the name of a valiant ancestor, and clans grouped into tribes, with shifting, wary alliances tied to grazing and water rights. The Bedu became proudly independent groups, quick to take offence but adhering to astonishingly strict codes of behaviour, scornful of pain and danger and intensely proud of their different ancestries.

The Bedouin call the camel *ata Allah*, God's gift. It was all that God gave them, and it was enough. A camel

Desert society centres around the camp fire. Under the strict rules of Bedouin hospitality, a stranger must be made welcome and fed for three days before it is proper to start asking questions.

Whether reduced to rags or richly robed, the Bedouin of Arabia carries himself with haughty pride. He can recite his lineage back many generations and is so secure within himself that he has little awe of the phenomenally changed world around him.

The dry, greenish coffee beans are roasted in a shallow pan. As the aroma begins to rise, the beans – now pale brown – are tossed into a heavy brass mortar and pounded with a pestle that chimes an invitation to any man within earshot. Cardamom seed is sprinkled in, pounded, and the mix tipped into a coffeepot of boiling water. The pot is brought back to the boil three times before a palm fibre is poked up the spout to act as strainer for the greeny-brown liquid poured carefully into minute cups. It is seemly for a guest to drink three cupfuls of the strong and bitter beverage before overturning his cup to signal satisfaction.

Eulogised by generations of poets and mystics, the rose of Taif fills the homes of Saudi Arabia's unofficial summer capital with its perfume and gaiety. Taif is only 45 miles from Mecca, but is perched 5000 feet up amid brown crags cut through with high valleys in which almond trees, apricots and pomegranates flourish.

This is a corner of old Abha, capital of the Asir, a rugged tableland that thrusts nearly a mile and a half above the steamy heat of the narrow Red Sea coastal plain.

can go without water for up to six weeks in winter, and for several days in the height of summer. More important is its ability to convert scraggy vegetation and the most brackish, foul water into rich milk, staple of the Bedouin diet. On special occasions, when a young male camel is roasted for a feast, nothing is wasted. The hair is made into rope and cloth, the skin into water bags; the dung becomes fuel, the urine serves as shampoo, as eyewash, as antiseptic for wounds, and even as a purgative.

As haughty as they were once poor, the prickly, proud Bedouin have traditionally bowed to no one. Their tribal sheikh was no more than the first among equals: he ruled through arbitration, and only so long as he commanded respect. Tents make inadequate prisons, so justice had to be swift and severe to be a deterrent.

Loyalty was at the core of *asabiyya,* clan spirit; betrayal the worst sin of all. Generosity in the form of hospitality to wanderers was another cardinal rule of the desert. Honour was a collective matter: the shame of one was the disgrace of all, and had to be avenged; thus blood feuds developed between tribes. The Bedouins' only high art was their eloquence, born of a rich, melodic, language that evolved around the camp fires, and bards spun reality into epic poetry that could inspire a raiding party and abash a foe. 'Lawful magic', the Saudis call Arabic.

The way of the desert was to become the way of Islam and, through Moorish Spain, became the inspiration for medieval chivalry. To harm the women, for example, was against the rules of raiding, yet women were as much chattled as cherished in this man's world. Their essential purpose was to produce the male children on which clan fortunes depended. In lean years, newborn females were buried alive, until the Prophet Muhammad, put a stop to it.

The winds of paradise

Islam means 'submission', and a Muslim is one who submits to the will of God and accepts God's word as revealed to Muhammad ibn Abdullah ibn Abd al-Muttalib ibn Hashim, a respected 7th-century merchant of Mecca, then a thriving, rowdy oasis at the junction of Arabia's major caravan routes, and a focus of pagan worship. Muhammad became distressed by Meccan morals, and retreated into the desert to meditate. There he experienced the first of a series of visions, which he interpreted as the word of God (Allah in Arabic) revealed to him by the archangel Gabriel, and which he relayed in passages of rich, rhyming prose called *surahs.* These surahs together make up the Koran, which means 'recitation' in Arabic.

When Muhammad called upon the Meccans to surrender themselves to one almighty and compassionate God, they suspected it might be bad for business, and turned on Muhammad. He fled for his life to Yathrib (now Medina), where he hoped for a better reception from its many Jewish traders and farmers. His

It is more than 60 years since the last Bedouin raid, but the fiery spirit of the old days is embodied in this member of the king's personal bodyguard, drawn exclusively from tribes that fought alongside the al-Saud in their rise to power.

The fortress houses of the Asir are set amid small terraced fields that catch the run-off from the rains of the Indian Ocean monsoon. The air this high is crisp, and the mountaintops are clothed with fragrant junipers.

Two young gentlemen squat diffidently in the majlis *(reception room), a male preserve in the Saudi home that corresponds to the guest tent of the nomad. The younger boy will don the ankle-length* thobe *and* ghutra *headdress of manhood after his circumcision. The bright wall colours and geometric patterns are an old tradition in central Arabian villages.*

flight (known as the *Hegira*) took place on September 24, AD 622 – later marked as the beginning of the Islamic calendar. When the Jews refused to accept him as their new prophet, Muhammad modified the practice of Islam to make it distinctively Arab. But when he declared holy war (*jihad*) on non-believers, he instructed followers to spare Jews and Christians as 'people of the book' who shared the one God. By January 630, he was back in Mecca, destroying its idols; his followers swept on, and oasis by oasis, made Islam the desert way of life.

Muhammad died in June 632, but the conquest had only begun. The Bedouin overflowed from the Arabian peninsula as an unstoppable force of holy warriors, known to their startled enemies as Saracens. Within 100 years a vast crescent from India to Spain had been conquered for the new faith. The fulcrum of Islam consequently shifted from the desert to Baghdad, then Constantinople, and Arabia turned in upon itself once more, to become a backwater of the Ottoman Empire. It was not until the 18th century that the desert threw up a reformer as austere as itself.

Muhammad ibn Abd al Wahhab was a fundamentalist *qadi* (judge) enraged by religious backsliding. He interpreted the Koran in the strictest way possible, and set the new tone by having a woman stoned to death for adultery. He banned shaving, smoking, music, dancing, even whistling (alcohol and gambling being already proscribed by the Prophet), and went about smashing anything that smacked of a graven image. When he found a sponsoring sheikh in 1744, he declared holy war on all who rejected his puritan ways. The sheikh's name was Muhammad ibn Saud. The Wahhabi-Saud alliance – continued by Muhammad ibn Saud's descendants – captured Mecca and Medina in the first years of the 19th century, turning away pilgrims as idolaters until an army was dispatched from Cairo to put down the uprising.

The great-great grandfather of the founder of Saudi Arabia was captured in 1818 and taken in chains to Constantinople, where his head was lopped off and crushed in a mortar, but this did not crush desert fundamentalism. It was with a force of Wahhabi zealots known as the Ikhwan (Brethren) that Abdul Aziz ibn Saud carved out the modern kingdom after his recapture of Riyadh in 1902. The Brethren took no prisoners, and charged to the kill with the war cry: 'The winds of Paradise are blowing.'

Their task accomplished, the Brethren were disbanded, and a few of those who rose in baffled rage against the new restrictions, as well as the king's use of certain innovations – car, wireless, telephone – not authorised by God in the Koran, were slaughtered by another device of Satan, the machine gun. Yet Wahhabism itself did not perish. It is the official form of Islam in Saudi Arabia today, and the royal house of Saud continues to intermarry with descendants of Muhammad ibn Abd al Wahhab, 'The Teacher'.

In the name of God

The flag of Saudi Arabia is the same as the green banner that the al-Saud bore streaming into battle at the head of a thousand camel-mounted holy warriors. Inscribed upon it is the creed of Islam: 'There is no god but God. And Muhammad is the messenger of God.' Bismallah – 'In the name of God' – is the affirmation that tops every government document; it appears on the television test card; it is intoned at take-off by Saudi airline pilots; computers throw it up at the start of each print-out. Foreign residents are, of course, permitted in Saudi Arabia, but even among them there is a sharp distinction between Muslims and non-Muslims: your religion is clearly stated in Arabic in your passport if you are travelling in the country on a visitor's visa; your residence permit, if you have one, will be white if you are a Muslim, brown if you are not.

Devout Saudis see the hand of God in the train of events beginning on March 16, 1938, when American prospectors struck oil on the Arabian Gulf coast, near a huddle of palm-frond shacks that went by the name of Dhahran. The population then amounted to perhaps half a million tribesmen and their camels, living under conditions similar to those of their Old Testament forebears. The Kingdom's few sources of wealth was the gold in the king's saddlebags. Today Saudi Arabia has one of the highest per capita incomes in the world, and employs a huge expatriate work force of Yemenis, Pakistanis, Egyptians, Filipinos and Westerners to attend to menial and technical needs.

Despite this, Islam continues to be practised the rigorous Wahhabi way. For 20 minutes, five times each day, everything shuts down as the entire nation drops to its knees to pray in the direction of the Kaaba in Mecca. During the fasting month of Ramadan no Westerners dare be seen between dawn and dusk sneaking a sip of water or a cigarette lest they be reported to the *matawain,* the religious police, zealots who dye their beards with henna and wield camel whips. There are no bars, discos, nightclubs, or cinemas in Saudi Arabia. Even videotape imports of *The Muppet Show* were barred from the kingdom, because its heroine was a pig. Dating is as illicit as alcohol. Persistent thieves have their hands chopped off. Murderers and rapists are executed, and the penalty for adultery (though rarely exacted) is death by stoning in the public square after noon prayers on Fridays. Saudi women go cloaked and veiled, segregated at all times from men other than their fathers, husbands, sons and other close relatives. Western women also have to watch their dress. Few bother to wear veils, or even cover their heads, in cities such as Jeddah or Riyadh, but in smaller places it is safer for them to cover their heads at least, and in some places local authorities will demand that they go veiled as well.

The forbidden cities

Mecca and Medina are among the last remaining forbidden cities on earth, both strictly off limits to non-Muslims – the roads leading to both have fearsome checkpoints, and non-Muslims who get even this close are fined. Mecca lies in a series of hot, wide valleys, sunk beneath harsh hills that deny travellers on the Christian Bypass even a binocular peek. So it is a surprise to discover that Mecca has red double-decker buses just like London, flyovers, high-rise office blocks, supermarkets, car parks, and luxury hotels.

More than 2 million Muslims from all over the world converge here for the annual *hajj* (pilgrimage), a momentous occasion televised by satellite to 47 countries, with the prayers broadcast in seven languages. Rich, royal, or dirt-poor, all become indistinguishable, the men wrapping themselves in shroud-like white *ihram* cloths, the women in white *abayas,* for an arduous 20-mile perambulation of sites associated with Abraham and Muhammad.

The constant threat of epidemic once plagued the *hajj,* but the Saudis have poured huge amounts of their oil wealth into pilgrim welfare. There are now quarantine hospitals, a sea terminal and an enormous airport at Jeddah, as well as a soaring fibreglass reception centre half a mile square – the largest enclosed space anywhere – and an eight-lane motorway into Mecca, 50 miles away.

The marble-walled courtyard of the Grand Mosque in Mecca can accommodate more than 300,000 people at prayer. It is dominated by the Kaaba, the spiritual centre of Islam. Neither temple nor shrine, this stark stone cube stands empty as the day when Muhammad cast out the idols; a symbol of the abstract oneness of God. Embedded in a corner is the Black Stone. The faithful believe it to be a relic of a structure built by Abraham

The gold and silver door of the Kaaba guards an empty interior. The pilgrimage to this epicentre of the Islamic faith was once frowned upon by puritanical Saudi zealots, but now the government lavishes billions of dollars on pilgrim care. The stone-and-mortar Kaaba is draped in black silk into which the name of God is intricately worked in gold thread.

Harvesting the desert is another Saudi miracle – but an expensive one. Near the oasis of al-Kharj, 50 miles south of Riyadh, huge sprinklers delivering water and liquid fertiliser at 1250 gallons a minute helped the kingdom to become self-sufficient in wheat, but grain produced this way costs up to ten times as much as imports.

Strawberries ripen under protective cover that enables all manner of fruit and vegetables to thrive in an intemperate land. The audacious agricultural programme has been a means of distributing oil wealth to remote areas.

Falconry is the national pastime of Saudi Arabia, despite recent inroads made by soccer. Royal parties with glinty-eyed birds of prey hunt the desert in specially converted Range Rovers, maintaining good relations with the desert tribesmen while they pursue their sport.

on the spot where God tested him with demands that he sacrifice his son Ismael (the Bible opts for another son, Isaac). Tradition holds that the stone was cast down by God to Adam as a sign of reconciliation after the expulsion from the Garden of Eden. Sceptics take it to be a meteorite.

No pilgrim ever forgets the first glimpse of the Kaaba. 'I became suddenly dazed', an American Muslim wrote. 'My wife clung to my arm, trembling and sobbing. My daughter shuddered as if an electric current had shot through her, and my son was speechless.' The chanting pilgrims circle the Kaaba seven times, at each circuit raising their right hands to the Black Stone; those within range struggle to touch and kiss it. Many are in tears.

'Eternal values endure, even as the world changes', stresses an official from the Ministry of Pilgrimage. 'We apply the new technologies to further Islam.' A refrigeration plant and a computerised distribution system help to cope with enormous numbers of sheep and goats ritually slaughtered as part of the pilgrimage. Other innovations include banks of closed-circuit TV monitors, and helicopter-assisted crowd control. Security has been a priority since November 1979, when hundreds died in a two-week siege after religious fanatics seized the Grand Mosque. Sixty-three rebels captured alive were beheaded. Now vehicles entering Mecca are inspected for arms as well as infidels.

Medina, 250 miles up the motorway, is relaxed by comparison with Mecca. Scholars come to pore over

Muhammad considered building a 'most unprofitable thing that eateth up the wealth of the believer', but this is one opinion of the Prophet that the Saudis have chosen to disregard in their helter-skelter quest for new architectural forms.

rare Islamic texts, and the *hajjis* from many lands who have settled here lend it a quiet, cosmopolitan air. The gentler pace of development has left undisturbed the quaint old Ottoman architecture; the narrow cobblestone streets of Aguwat, the former Eunuchs' Quarter, overlooked by wooden balconies, might be in Istanbul.

Muhammad preferred Medina to Mecca and died here, aged 63, in the year 632. The Prophet's Mosque is a low brick enclosure with elegant minarets and a sunny courtyard. Pilgrims stand, palms raised in prayer, before his green-draped bier, which is protected behind grillwork. Mindful of the fundamental tenet of their religion, they pray for Muhammad, never to him.

The magic kingdom

'The magic kingdom' – that was how Western engineers and contract managers, in half-mocking wonder, described the turmoil of Saudi Arabia in the 1970s, when soaring oil prices increased national income by several thousand per cent. This caused such worldwide inflation that the Saudis determined the only solution to be to spend the money as fast as they got it – 200 billion dollars in a five-year plan dubbed 'an experiment in social transformation', to be followed by 400 billion dollars in the next five years. A people who a generation earlier had no word for million were sudden beneficiaries of the greatest transfer of wealth in history. It was also part of the process of modernisation. 'Like it or not, we must join the modern world and find an honourable place in it', King Faisal had said after he came to the throne in 1964. 'Revolution can come from thrones as well as from conspirators' cellars.'

Loaded freighters were queuing in the Red Sea halfway to Suez, waiting six months for a berth in clogged Jeddah, while a column of lorries stretching from Europe to the Gulf hauled overland everything from razor blades to ready-to-assemble docks. Such was

Saudi Arabia's first oil strike produced 2130 barrels on March 16, 1938, and the well is still pumping today. As much as a third of total world oil reserves lie under the kingdom's deserts and Gulf coast waters. They include the world's largest oil field, Ghanwar, and the largest offshore field, Safaniya.

The hunt for more oil has ranged deep into The Empty Quarter. The sauntering camel and the exploration rig neatly encapsulate the Saudi story, past and present.

The water truck is the lifeline of Saudi Arabia. As with oil, large reservoirs of fresh water were found deep under the desert, some up to 30,000 years old. These are being depleted at an alarming rate. Sea water can be desalinated at great expense, but some visionaries speak of one day towing icebergs from the Antarctic.

the need and urgency of development that cement was helicoptered off the waiting ships, and herds of dairy cows were imported from America by air. Riyadh disappeared under the rubble of its own re-creation, while property prices doubled by the week.

The pace of change was remarkable indeed. Just 40 years earlier one important sheikh, a friend of King Abdul Aziz, had found the wireless too much to take, holding stoutly to the belief that the kingdom's new radio stations were kept running solely by regular visits from Satan himself. The king had only been able to convince his friend otherwise by establishing radio contact with the Great Mosque in Riyadh and getting the imam there to read out the first verses of the Koran – thus proving that the new device could carry God's word and must therefore have divine sanction.

Now, in the 1970s, large numbers of the Saudi male population were making the leap from camel to the car – literally so in a sufficient number of instances for the Toyota dealership in Riyadh to provide a camel pen. The consequence was carnage on a grand scale. 'A charge of ridden camels going nearly 30 miles an hour was irresistible', Lawrence of Arabia had discovered when fighting with the Bedouin, and the Saudis rode their cars like their camels. The number of wrecked or abandoned cars littering the burgeoning city by the following year was estimated at 80,000. By February 1980, an international survey had named Jeddah the world's most expensive city, yet that same month the municipality rounded up 4350 sheep and goats left to stray in the streets. When the dust partially settled with the ending of the oil boom, a new – but fundamentally unchanged – Saudi Arabia was revealed.

Cities in the sand

T.E. Lawrence (Lawrence of Arabia) wrote of Jeddah: 'The white town hung between the blazing sky and its reflection which swept and rolled over the wide lagoon. The heat of Arabia came like a drawn sword and struck us speechless.' The sweltering little port at a break in the Red Sea coral reef was what passed for the commercial hub of pre-petroleum Arabia. Dates, gold

The mud walls of old Riyadh are besieged by alien invaders such as the television tower. The modern Saudi capital sprang up in such a speedy, erratic fashion that patches of desert are encountered between populated areas.

Camels are traffic hazards that need to be marshalled away from the new motorways. A single Mercedes truck can haul in a two-day desert crossing what a 130-camel caravan over the same route took 50 to 60 days to carry.

and slaves were the staples of trade in the Prophet's day, and only in 1962 were the last slaves freed. The picturesque merchant houses of coral and teak still dance in the heat haze, but the merchants have moved out to the tall office blocks that now hem in the Old Town. As the commercial hub of an oil superpower, Jeddah – a complex of ring roads and flyovers, shopping malls and private palaces – now sprawls over 150 square miles of the narrow coastal plain.

Jeddah assembles the Mercedes trucks that are the new ships of the desert. Each one has the capacity of a large camel caravan, and is 50 times as fast. They rumble over the 500 miles to Riyadh, beloved beasts painted with bright geometric designs or scenes of the lush Islamic paradise. Sometimes there are loudspeakers mounted outside, deafening the desert with taped music.

Riyadh is the colour of the desert from which it sprang: every tone of beige from white to brown. Its name means 'gardens', after the date groves and wells of the Wadi Hanifa in which it lies. Its distinctive feature, appropriately, is a flared water tower that hovers like a flying saucer over squat mud remnants of the age before oil. As much as the oil, Riyadh depends for its survival upon large reservoirs of water discovered deep underground. The homes of wealthy businessmen and royalty have the size and sometimes the appearance of resort hotels. However, there is a disjointed look about so much modern architecture, bad, good, or simply surprising; one house actually rotates with the sun.

One big tribe

Saudi Arabia is a theocratic monarchy, ruled by a king who is its religious leader, prime minister, and commander-in-chief. It has no elections; political parties are illegal; and there is no freedom of religion, or any of the other freedoms generally taken for granted in the West. Instead, it has the Sharia, the Law of God as defined by a medieval interpretation of the Koran, and it has the al-Saud. 'The al-Saud family is Saudi Arabia. They decide who can enter or leave the country, who will become rich or poor, and who lives or dies', wrote one American commentator.

Saudi Arabia can be likened to a Bedouin tribe, with the al-Saud as the sheikhly family-in-charge. Four sons of Abdul Aziz have succeeded their father, chosen in secret conclave by an inner circle of leading family members, in close consultation with the *ulema*, the all-powerful religious scholars. The first, King Saud, a weak profligate who brought the kingdom to the brink

The aggal, *the black double headcord worn over the* ghutra *(headdress), originated as a rope tether for camels. This city gentleman's family may have sold their last camel generations ago, but with government encouragement the comfort of traditional Saudi dress has remained popular.*

of bankruptcy, was obliged by family and *ulema* to abdicate in favour of Faisal, his astute, austere half-brother. Faisal led the kingdom to unimagined wealth only to be assassinated by a nephew, possibly in revenge for the shooting to death of another nephew during a fundamentalist demonstration against the introduction of television. Faisal was followed by gentle, kindly Khalid, who forsook the gold-wire *aggal* for the plain black headcords of traditional Saudi dress, and who most enjoyed hunting with his falcons among the desert Bedouin. Khalid died in 1982, and was succeeded by the worldly Fahd ('leopard'), an experienced administrator. One day the al-Saud will run out of ibn (son of) Abdul Azizs, but not soon; dozens remain, the youngest turning 50 in 1997.

Like true sheikhs, the king and senior princes hold regular *majlises* (audiences) when they receive a trail of subjects seeking favours. In the old days, the *majlis* was one of the most important and characteristic institutions of Bedouin tribal organisation, where the sheikh and his followers exchanged news about the activities of rival tribes, gave each other information about any good pasture they had found for their herds and flocks, and decided where to move on to next. The 19th-century Englishman Charles M. Doughty who spent two years in the 1870s wandering the desert with Bedouin tribespeople spoke highly of the practical democracy displayed on these occasions: 'Let him speak here who will,' he wrote in his classic *Travels in Arabia Deserta*, 'the voice of the least is heard among them; he is a tribesman.' He also praised the justice that the sheikhs administered at *majlises*: 'Hither the tribesmen may bring their causes at all times, and it is pleaded by the maintainers of both sides with busy clamour; and everyone may say his word that will. The sheikh meanwhile takes counsel . . . and judgment is given commonly without partiality and always without bribes. This sentence is final. The loser is mulcted in heads of small cattle or camels, which he must pay anon, or go into exile.' And yet in spite of such swift justice, many Bedouin were reluctant to pay up: 'The poor Bedouins are very unwilling payers, . . . thus, in every tribe, some households may be seen of other tribes' exiles.'

The shapeless silhouette beloved by Western cartoonists is the Saudi response to Koranic insistence on female modesty. Beneath her black abaya *and veil, this supermarket shopper might be wearing T-shirt and jeans, or the latest designer wear from Paris.*

Riyadh University aspires to become the best in the Arab world. To this end, the government spent 5 billion dollars on this new campus.

Only the Koran was taught in Saudi Arabia until the 1940s. The first girls' school opened in 1956 – disguised as an orphanage.

The Turkish-style teakwood mashrabiyyah *balconies of the old merchants' houses in Jeddah were crafted to catch any breeze, while their latticework allowed the women a vantage point without being seen. The thick walls of porous coral rag moderate the temperature even in the torrid summer.*

The streets of Jeddah are livelier than those of staid Riyadh, especially near the Bab al-Yeman ('door of Yeman') Market where everything from jewellery to vegetables is sold. Men squat before their shops puffing on long-stemmed pipes.

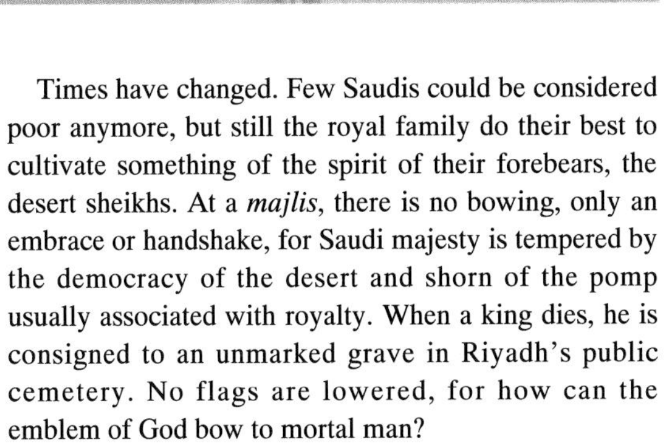

Times have changed. Few Saudis could be considered poor anymore, but still the royal family do their best to cultivate something of the spirit of their forebears, the desert sheikhs. At a *majlis*, there is no bowing, only an embrace or handshake, for Saudi majesty is tempered by the democracy of the desert and shorn of the pomp usually associated with royalty. When a king dies, he is consigned to an unmarked grave in Riyadh's public cemetery. No flags are lowered, for how can the emblem of God bow to mortal man?

The business of marriage

Family loyalty is a lifelong obligation for a Saudi. Three generations often share the same home, and other relatives will live nearby. The selection of a wife is a serious matter. As it was in the desert, a first cousin is sometimes the first choice, though marriages to more distant cousins are more common now and a good 50 per cent of them marry non-relatives. When the right bride is found, hard bargaining by the parents ensues. The prospective groom must pay her a substantial *mahr* (dower), usually gold coins and jewellery, her security in case of divorce.

With little public entertainment (even soccer was frowned upon by many of the *ulema*, until Saudi Arabia won the Asia Cup), families make their own. Streets come alive once the sun goes down, families spreading rugs, chatting and playing cards, or visiting the *souks* (bazaars). On Fridays, city families often drive into the desert to picnic. Saudis also love to visit, and coffee drinking is the prime social ritual in cities as much as in

The souk *moneychanger riffling through wads of dollar bills, pound notes, Swiss francs and Saudi riyals is a familiar sight in a land where the Koran's injunction against usury delayed the development of banks. Saudi Arabia had no paper money of its own until well into the 1950s.*

the desert. The coffee, which is bitter, very strong and spiced deliciously with cardamom seeds, is drunk from small cups without handles, and a polite host will keep topping the cups up unless guests indicate that they have had enough.

The traditional Bedouin feast is another delight that has made the transition to the cities. The main dish is often a whole roast lamb served on a bed or pilaf rice mixed with raisins and pine nuts; and there may be mutton, chicken, goat or camel. Guests sit on the ground and help themselves with one hand – the right. Soups and salads will also feature, and may be flavoured with chives, coriander or dill. A variety of fish is available, too, in coastal regions; *shami* or *samul* bread is eaten, as with every meal. Finally, dates are a traditional sweet, though there may also be *muhallabiyah*, a milk pudding, and the sticky *kneifah* or *bakhlava*, a kind of pastry filled with honey and nuts.

Though a man is permitted up to four wives at a time so long as they are treated with strict impartiality, monogamy is the norm. A man can still, however, get a divorce virtually on demand. Equally, though, Sharia law is vigilant in protecting female property and inheritance rights.

The black veil symbolises to Westerners the subjugation of Saudi women. So what should visitors make of a recent adaptation: the designer veil, coyly edged in gold with the signature of some famous couturier? Education is free to any Saudi girl whose family permits it, and thousands of women now have university degrees. Some are doctors, social workers, bankers, engineers, businesswomen, but they must organise it so that they do not come into direct contact with men. 'If a man and a woman are alone in one place,' goes the proverb, 'the third person present is Satan.' So there are women's banks, women's souks, stout walls and separate doors in government offices, and girl students receive their lectures by closed-circuit TV. No woman in Saudi Arabia is allowed a driving licence, nor can she travel alone in a taxi, board a plane, or stay in a hotel without the written consent of a male relative. When 47 Saudi women in a convoy of 14 cars attempted to go for a drive in Riyadh in November 1990, all were quickly arrested, and 20,000 angry men attended a demonstration to protest against this female outrage.

A Saudi woman is answerable to her family in the person of the senior male, the custodian of family honour (this is true even of married women who are answerable to the senior male of their family of birth rather than to their husband). What this can mean was demonstrated by the execution in 1977 of Princess Mishaal and her lover. The princess was married, and the pair were attempting to slip out of the country when caught. Her grandfather, Muhammad ibn Saud, was an arch-traditionalist who reacted with the fury of a desert patriarch. The princess was led out to a car park in Jeddah, and made to kneel down before a pile of sand. She was then shot six times in the head while her lover, a student named Khalid Muhalhal, watched. The student was then beheaded with a scimitar wielded by a member of the princess's family.

The sitting room of this businessman reflects universal middle-class tastes, but the absence of women marks it as Saudi. Few Saudis consider it proper for women to be photographed, even in their own homes.

Yemen

The geographers of the ancient world divided Arabia into Arabia Deserta (desert Arabia) and Arabia Felix (happy Arabia). Arabia Felix was a land blessed by the gods, abundantly watered and producing incense and highly valued aromatic spices. Today, it corresponds roughly to Yemen, its green mountains bordered by deserts, its shores studded with the ports of the old trade routes between West and East. Until recently, the vagaries of history had left it divided into two countries. Now united, Yemen brings together people as varied as the merchants of Aden and the coastal cities, and the tribespeople of the high interior and the Hadramawt valley.

The fortress-like villages of the Harraz blend so completely into their surroundings that it is often impossible to tell where mountain ends and village begins.

Previous page:
Female dress codes in Yemen are bewildering in their variety and contradictions. In many areas, women are veiled or masked, but not in the southern Hajaaz, where this woman of Jebel Bura' flashes a proud smile under a stylish loose turban.

The more precipitous and picturesque the setting, the harder the task of the village women, who have constantly to fetch water and firewood and feed for the family cow. They commonly carry loads of 50 pounds or more on their heads for long distances up the steepest slopes.

The Roof of Arabia

In Roman times, this elbow of mountainous terrain nudging the Red Sea and the Gulf of Aden was known as Arabia Felix – Happy Arabia – a corner of fertility in a desert continent. It was from here that the great camel trains came, loaded with frankincense and myrrh, silks, pearls, silver and gold.

The Bible mentions the most famous of the caravans – the one that brought the Queen of Sheba to Jerusalem 'with camels that [did] bear spices, and very much gold, and precious stones...There came no more such abundance of spices as these which the Queen of Sheba gave to King Solomon.' Though Solomon had 700 wives and 300 concubines (according to the count in the First Book of Kings), this visitor really turned the royal eye if, as scholars deduce, the Song of Solomon ('Yea, thou are fair, my love; yea, thou art fair; thou hast dove's eyes...') is based upon their meeting.

The Bible fails to give the queen a name, but in the Koran she is identified as Bilqis. The Koran tells how the mighty and wise Sulaiman (Solomon in Arabic) heard of a wonderful green land in the south ruled by a queen who worshipped the sun instead of God, and he sent a migrating hoopoe bird with a letter warning her to desist from her heathen ways. Queen Bilqis was intrigued, and dispatched an envoy with riddles to test Solomon's wisdom; impressed by the response, she journeyed north and, just as in the Bible, was converted to God. The legend was greatly embellished through the centuries – nowhere more than in Ethiopia, whose Christian emperors were said to be descended from Solomon and the Queen of Sheba through a son, Menelik, who was conceived during the famous visit. The last emperor, Haile Selassie, made this an article of the constitution.

Sheba – or Saba – was for more than a thousand years the most important of the southern Arabian kingdoms, the ancestral state to which all Yemenis (from a word meaning south) like to trace their origins. It was placed in the crook of the mountainous elbow, on the axis of trails feeding into the main route north to the Mediterranean, two months away when all went well. The caravans sometimes comprised of thousands of camels. Saba's pride was a great dam built around 800 BC – a century after Solomon and Bilqis. It straddled a gorge and trapped enough run-off from the mountain rains for thousands of acres of the desert margins to be cultivated and the largest caravans to be provisioned.

The Koran records the end of the Sabaeans, ascribing the collapse of their dam in AD 570 (the year of Muhammad's birth) to heavenly wrath: the people had turned aside from God, 'so we unleashed upon them the flood waters...and we changed them their lush gardens into gardens bearing bitter fruit, tamarisks and here and there a lote-tree.' Saba's decline had begun as early as the 1st century AD, when navigators discovered how to use the monsoons as reliable trade winds that blew their ships down the Red Sea and all the way to India every summer, and brought them home again in the winter. Just as sea trade broke the caravan monopoly, the rise of Christianity reduced demand for pagan ritual fragrances such as frankincense, the staple of the overland trade. A weakened Saba fell twice under the Ethiopians, and the great dam broke and was laboriously repaired several times before its final collapse. Other strongholds along the caravan route suffered much the same decline, hastened by Bedouin tribes made belligerent by their loss of tribute, and the Yemen became a backwater of rival dynasties and tribes united only by an allegiance to the new faith of Islam.

Most important were the Zaidi Imams, leaders of a local Muslim sect – a branch of the shiite form of Islam – founded by a descendant of the prophet. The autocratic Imams ruled parts of the Yemen, sometimes under Ottoman Turkish overlords, for 1065 years – right up to the 1962 revolution, when this was one of the most antique places on earth, trapped in the early Middle Ages, with no paved roads and with disease rampant. In the south, the port of Aden was a British

The now-rare mountain goat is sought for its horns, which decorate some rooftops from Yemen to Afghanistan. The custom is pre-Islamic, its origins lost in time.

Tihami youngsters in the region's distinctive straw hats drive the family sheep to rocky pastures in foothills above the Red Sea coast. Sheep are in such demand for the annual Eid al-Kebir feast commemorating Abraham's sacrifice that some have to be imported from Somalia.

The Yemeni camel – especially those of Al-Mahra in the eastern desert – have a reputation for endurance that dates back more than 2000 years to the heyday of the caravans. The clay houses of the desert margins have stone foundations that provide protection from the rare wadi flood.

bastion from 1839, with a buffer of numerous small protectorates that Whitehall left largely to themselves. By the late 1960s, a decade of growing nationalism and enduring tribal rivalry had created two independent, warring Yemens, a militantly Marxist People's Democratic Republic where the British and their protectorates had been, and a Western-backed Yemen Arab Republic in place of the medieval Imamate.

As early as 1979 the leaders of the two republics made a commitment to merge their countries, but assassinations and power struggles kept putting it off. Only in May 1990 did unification finally come into being, with a five-member Presidential Council left in charge until democratic elections due to be held at the end of 1992.

The rains of the desert

This is the story told soberly, but Yemen defies sober analysis. Even the Queen of Sheba cannot be pinned down as an authentic historical figure, for no mention of her has been found in the ancient inscriptions that litter the caravan route: rather, she is thought to be an amalgamation of fact and ideal, just as she is to Yemenis the embodiment of lost glory.

They need such a heroine, for since its abrupt entry into the modern world Yemen's image has suffered. The rot set in with Evelyn Waugh, who in 1930 examined the Yemenis and was characteristically disparaging. 'They are of small stature and meagre muscular development', he wrote. 'Their faces are hairless or

seems to match, but is defiantly different, from the fairy-tale sandcastle houses to the sartorial jumble of the citizen-warrior's curved dagger, *futah* skirt and sports jacket. It comes with the topography, for Yemen has one of the most varied and rugged landscapes in Arabia.

The cracking and buffeting of the earth's crust that caused the great slab of Arabia to break loose from the land masses of both Africa and Asia also left it on a tilt: the entire peninsula is on a distinct slope from west to east. The top of the tilt is in the extreme south-west, where the jagged Harraz mountains reach 12,336 feet at the summit of Hadur Shu'ayb. This is a sufficient barrier to trap humid summer winds drifting off the Indian Ocean, pushing them upwards so that they cool and dump their moisture. This happens in sudden downpours, which course down the steep slopes and surge along wadis carved through the millennia until every drop has disappeared into the parched ground, usually well short of the sea.

The rains are as fitful as they are violent, the downpours so localised that a road may be washed away while a village a few hundred yards down the track stays bone dry. Some years, there may be no rain at all; there were several severe droughts in the 1980s. To call this a monsoon is as misleading as to call these mountains the Switzerland of Arabia, and the popular phrase 'Green Arabia' is a relative term, but it is enough to make a world of difference. The lowlands bordering the Red Sea and the Gulf of Aden may be as hot and torrid as anywhere in Arabia, but in the highlands of the interior temperatures rarely exceed 20°C (70°F) even in

A mud mason demonstrates the zabur *technique of house construction used in the northern town of Sa'dah. Clods of a mud-straw mix are flung to him by helpers who time their actions to a musical rhythm. Layers are applied slowly and with great care, each one very slightly in from the previous one, so that walls lean into one another to improve stability; a smooth finish is then applied.*

This building in Tarim is constructed of mud brick moulded in wooden frames and air-dried. Mud structures are resistant to the brief heavy deluges characteristic of Yemen, but would not stand up to light, persistent rain that seeps in faster than the sun can burn it off.

covered with a slight down, their expressions degenerate and slightly dotty, an impression which is accentuated by their loping, irregular gait.' The commentaries did not improve. Communist South Yemen was inaccessible, except to airline hijackers and political terrorists on the run. The few travellers to the North brought back tales of men brandishing Kalashnikov rifles and living in a trance, sustained by munching on the leaves of a narcotic bush, called qat, that looked and tasted like privet hedge. Arabia Felix had evidently become Arabia Demens.

Now, with the opening up of the country, Yemen stands revealed in all its confusions. The rest of the peninsula is a monochrome of conformity – white robes, white headdresses, sandals and sand. In Yemen, nothing

Qat chewing is a national habit in Yemen. The juicy green leaves must be fresh for fullest effect, so supplies are rushed each morning to qat markets in every town and village. Prices vary greatly according to quality and location.

summer, and in winter snow and frost are common. The higher altitudes are capable of producing rich crops of cereals, fruits (among them wonderfully succulent desert grapes) and vegetables.

Presenting yet another face, meanwhile, is the island of Socatra – its name derived from the Sanskrit for 'island abode of bliss' – lying some 220 miles off mainland Yemen's south coast at the mouth of the Gulf of Aden. It consists mostly of a barren plateau rising to 4700 feet, but its narrow coastal plains and valleys produce harvests of dates as well as the incenses myrrh, frankincense and aloes. Also growing widely on the island are dragon's blood palms, so called because of their red resin, once employed medicinally, now chiefly used to colour varnishes and lacquers, especially those for violins. Socatra's 12,000 inhabitants are as exotic as its crops. Their mixed ancestry – Arab, African, Greek and Portuguese – bears witness to the island's key strategic position on the trade rourtes between East and West. They were Christians until the 17th century, since

A wife prepares the mada'a (hubble-bubble) without which no social gathering is complete. The women of the household are invisible hostesses, never seen by the male guests.

This relaxed scene in the Hadramawt has a worrying aspect. Yemeni families tend to be large, and the population is increasing at an alarming rate, even though infant mortality is still high.

when Islam has taken over as the dominant religion. Many islanders still speak a language akin to the ancient Himyarite tongue of pre-Islamic Arabia.

Beyond the Gate of Tears

Approached from the Red Sea, Yemen deceives by appearing at first to be an extension of Africa, which is only 30 miles away at the choke point on the Red Sea known as the Bab al Mandeb – the Gate of Tears. The narrow coastal strip is called the Tihama, which means 'hot earth', an accurate description. The humidity is intense, and the wind is laden with sand. A well, a sputtering pump, a clump of palms are reminders that life is possible. The people are generally darker, and often show traces of African ancestry, and the straw-roofed villages recall African kraals.

At the entrance to the Bab al Mandeb is Al Mukha, a ghostly reminder of another Yemeni trading monopoly, as forgotten now as that of frankincense. In the 17th century, the merchants of Mocha controlled the world trade in coffee, an exciting new beverage taking Europe by storm. Though wild coffee may have originated across the strait in Africa, it was first cultivated in the mountain ranges above Mocha, where the climatic conditions are ideal. European powers scrambled to set up trading posts here, but eventually they were able to smuggle young shrubs on to their ships, and soon coffee

These grizzled veterans of San'a have witnessed decades of revolution and internal strife which culminated in the political unification of the Yemen for the first time ever.

plantations dotted their colonies from Java to Jamaica, fatally undercutting the Yemenis. It was another case of boom to bust. The population of Mocha dropped from 20,000 to 400 in the 19th century, its famous port fallen into ruin, the trade name 'Mocha coffee' its only memorial. The Yemenis still grow coffee, but contrary as ever, they value the husk more highly, from which they brew *qishr,* an infusion often flavoured with ginger and cardamom.

The climb out of the steamy Tihama up narrow wadis is steep, the vegetation sparse and tropical: a patch of pink-bloomed euphorbias or sweetly fragrant kadhi, used by the Tihami to perfume their clothes, and nowadays small banana and papaya plantations. Along the way are *miqhayas,* roadhouses offering *qishr,* tea, soft drinks, and a place to doze off or to smoke the *mada'a* (hubble-bubble) on a *sarir,* a string bed. In a corner are stacks of wood, bags of coal, watermelons and bunches of bananas waiting to be trucked this way or that.

The temperature cools, the air freshens, and a few roads spiral upwards into the Harraz, where fortress villages cling to crags amid tiny stepped terraces; the mountainscape is a jigsaw of extraordinary ingenuity, created and maintained over thousands of years. Beyond the 10,000-foot passes lie the high plateaus, the most fertile, best-watered region of Arabia. The northern capital, San'a, lies in the heart of the region at just over 7000 feet. Eastward, the mountains sag to around 3000 feet, snagged here and there by the ruins of an incense city, until the rocky landscape peters out, as does Yemen, in the great sand desert of the Rub al Khali (the Empty Quarter).

The frankincense trail

The unification of Yemen makes it possible to discover the country by following the frankincense trade route. This headily aromatic resin has been valued since the times of the ancient Egyptians at least, both as an incense for use in religious worship and as a medicine – the ancients believed it could be used to cure a number of physical ailments. And the desert plateaus of southern Yemen are one of the few places in the world which grow the scrubby trees from which it is obtained; they are sufficiently high for heavy morning dews to provide the sparse sustenance the trees need. Frankincense itself comes from the milky juice produced when the trees' barks are slashed, later hardening into semi-transparent, yellow or greenish lumps.

The trail begins on the Gulf of Aden on a beach beneath a dark volcanic promontory known as Husn al-Ghurab, fortress of the raven. Dhows, nowadays diesel-powered, still ply the coast, but there is no hint that this was once Qana (Canneh in Ezekiel 27:23), a biblical port where cargoes of silk and spices from India and loads of incense rafted from points along the coast were assembled for the long journey north. In 1985, a research team pitched tents on the beach. Scooping out a pit for their camp fire, they detected a familiar scent. Digging deeper into the white sand, sure enough: 'The sweetness was there. Just barely. Frankincense!'

In the course of the Middle Ages, Qana was succeeded by Mukalla, along the coast, and this port did not die; it thrives today as a trade and fishing centre whose catches are exported as far as Sri Lanka. Crushed into its half-moon bay by steep and stark brown hills, Mukalla makes a pretty picture, the white houses with blue windows seeming to rise out of the sea, even if land reclamation and suburban growth are beginning to reduce the effect.

Mukalla architecture is a fascinating blend of Arab and Indian, and its culture a pot pourri of medieval and modern, Muhammad and Marx. The little city awakes to loudspeakers calling dawn prayers, followed by the wail of an Egyptian pop song beckoning early customers to the Freedom Café. The narrow street parallel to the sea is soon choked with small cars and trucks, while along the quay little cranes unload lighters. By noon prayertime, shutters are drawn and streets empty, as the blistering sun cooks up a staggering stench of dead shark and sewage; the ancients undoubtedly had practical as much as religious reasons for putting their trust in incense.

Aden is 400 miles to the west, along a coast road built in recent years by China as a gift. It is the cosmopolitan, visually uninspiring product of 128 years of British rule overlaid with two decades of Soviet tutelage, impressive only for its surroundings of volcanic peak and crater. As capital of the Arab world's only experiment in Marxism, its streets were strung with red banners proclaiming 'Glory to the People and the Party', but not much changed in the *souks* (markets),

Opposite: *The host sits at the centre of the back of the* mafraj *– best and highest room of the house – while friends settle down for the afternoon qat party. The conversation is animated at first, then slowly dies as the drug takes hold. The group will chew on an ever-larger wad of juicy leaves until sunset, intermittently taking puffs from the* mada'a *and quaffing copious amounts of coffee and tea to quench a qat-induced thirst.*

The curved dagger (jambiya) *worn by Yemeni men for at least 3000 years is not so much a weapon as a status symbol. By its style, workmanship, and the manner in which it is carried in the belt, much can be learned about the owner.*

where people went about their age-old ways as usual. Aden is the centre of what remains of the frankincense market, reduced to a tiny fraction of the 3000 tons estimated to have been dispatched annually for burning before the altars of ancient Greece and Rome. In tiny backrooms in the Souk al-Tam, however, women still chant as they clean and sort the dried resin.

From the torrid coast, the caravans clambered inland to the arid plateau of Jol, then tumbled into the isolated Wadi Hadramawt, the grandest ravine in all of Arabia, and a world of its own stretching 350 miles across eastern Yemen. Long before Islam arrived, the Hadramawt was the centre of an important kingdom; it now forms one of Arabia's most complex ethnic mosaics. There are around 1300 different tribes (many of them more like extended families) grouped into larger confederations, each intensely jealous of its ancient traditions and privileges, such as the partly nomadic Subaihi in the south-west and the Haushabi in the north. One of its chief towns is Sayun, the imposing mud-brick capital of Hadramawt Protectorate under the British, which calls itself 'the town of a million palm trees', and sports a colossal sultan's palace. Tarim, sited between palm groves and rock cliffs, claims to have as many mosques as there are days in the Muslim year (354...for 15,000 inhabitants!), and is a unique fusion of architectural styles, a sort of Oriental baroque, with rococo minarets, fluted columns, cornices and porticoes elegantly wrought by master mud masons.

The Hadramawt might appear to be as remote as any populated region of Arabia, yet looks always deceive in Yemen. Since the very first caravan, Yemenis have been inveterate travellers, and for centuries Hadrami men have left the valley to seek their fortunes abroad, particularly in the East Indies. Tarim is testimony to the many who made it. In contrast, there is nearby Shibam, the most spectacular settlement in Arabia. It consists of

The endangered Old City of San'a is a fragile architectural masterpiece, more like a stage set than home to 30,000 people.

Yemenis lovingly personalise their motorbikes, sometimes festooning them with flags, ribbons, flowers and feathers. Money earned working in Saudi Arabia and the Gulf oil states has transformed the people's expectations.

Mules and donkeys are an asset in Manakhan, a precipitous mountain town in the heart of the Harraz. The pattern on the wall beyond the alley is more than decorative – it helps to ward off evil.

What might appear to be the San'a chapter of the Hell's Angels is in fact a taxi rank. The motorbike cab can take only one fare at a time, but has the unique advantage of being able to burrow into the narrowest lane in the Old City.

500 tower blocks of six to eight storeys, stacked so tightly together that they form a single rampart rising from the bed of the wadi: the effect is eerily like a mirage of Manhattan. Shibam is testimony to the enduring qualities of mud brick: these tawny tenements are as much as 400 years old.

The caravan trail strikes north-west past thickets of myrrh, the other great incense bush, through defiles still used by the occasional camel train hauling salt to remote villages. It then moves out of the hills to skirt the south-western flank of the Empty Quarter, which at some point beyond the horizon becomes Saudi Arabia. Here, in a wadi that loses itself in the sands, is Marib, site of the fabled capital of the Queen of Sheba, and of the Sabaean kingdom that dominated the incense route for much of its history.

Jazzars – *butchers – are socially stigmatised and make up a subculture all of their own. Though such social barriers are breaking down, these youngsters may find difficulty obtaining any other kind of employment when they grow up, and are likely to marry within the* jazzar *group.*

Oil in the land of Sheba

Until a few years ago, Marib might easily have been recognised from the Koranic description of its fate. The broken dam can still be inspected at the desert end of the Wadi Adhana, a magnificent piece of ancient engineering that trapped the run-off from a catchment area of 10,000 square miles and irrigated some 60 square miles of palm-shaded gardens. God's curse has been lifted, for now at least. A few miles up the wadi, a new dam has been built with a 75-million dollar donation from Sheik Zaid bin Sultan al Nahayan of the United Arab Emirates, who traces his family to the Sabaean diaspora. Even before it had time to fill, water pumped from deep underground began to recreate the gardens of Sheba, producing fields of wheat and lemon groves bright with crested hoopoes, descendants of Solomon's messenger.

Old Marib is a ghost town, abandoned to the *hanesh* (puff adders), but a new Marib has shot up, brashly out

Jambiya blades are nowadays imported from Japan, but the most valued are still made by Yemeni craftsmen. Polishing is a separate craft, and so is hilt-carving. Hilts are commonly of cow horn, but the most prized are made from rhinoceros horn smuggled from Africa – a major reason why the rhino is threatened with extinction.*

of place in its stark modernity. A four-star hotel named after Queen Bilquis stands near the remains of a temple where she may have offered the sacrifices that irked Solomon. The explanation for this burst of activity is oil. In 1985, the Yemen Hunt Oil Company made the first of several strikes in the desert near here. Tentative plans call for half a million people to be settled in the district eventually, yet old ways die hard, and testy tribesmen are liable to take pot shots at oilmen's trucks.

It was certainly dangerous territory in the 1st century when the Roman scholar Pliny the Elder wrote that it was made 'a capital offence for a laden camel to leave the main road'. Things have changed little in this regard. Diplomats have speculated that there may be more arms per capita in the far north of Yemen than anywhere else on earth. After centuries of tribal conflict and decades of modern warfare, even a shepherd boy hereabouts is likely to be toting a Kalashnikov. Sa'dah, the northernmost town, was a fortified tribal stronghold closed to motor vehicles until as late as the 1970s, and at the open-air weapons market in the nearby village of Al-Talh (also noted for its basketware), grenades sold like tomatoes.

San'a – the fairy-tale city

San'a is not on the incense route, but high up within a cool, fertile bowl carved out of the western mountains, where the Sabaeans settled after the decline of the land route. The air is fresh, and thin enough to surprise visitors as they alight from their plane. Local legend recounts how San'a was founded by Shem, the eldest son of Noah, but inscriptions date it from about the time of Christ. For 1500 years the city on the rooftop of Arabia was certainly legendary to Europeans, who rarely ventured this far. As a result, San'a stayed untouched until the 1960s revolution, when the 50,000 people living within its thick mud walls bravely withstood a 70-day siege by Republican forces seeking

Even in the conservative north, young women sometimes wear Western clothes...at home. Out of doors, they envelope themselves in the sharshaf, *an all-black ensemble of Turkish origin that became fashionable with the upper class only in their grandmothers' time.*

Members of an Aden student folklore group in period costume act out what still comes naturally in other parts of Yemen. After 130 years of British rule, followed by its venture into Marxism, Aden is a cosmopolitan anomaly in a still largely tribal land.

to overthrow the newly acceded young Imam Muhammad al-Badr. Their bravery did not save the Imam, however. He was forced to flee into the remote north of the country where he led a vain resistance, with the support of Saudi Arabia, against the Egyptian-backed Republicans. The resulting civil war ended with full Republican victory in 1965.

Modern San'a has burst forth from its walls, repeatedly doubling in size; it entered the 1990s with a population of around half a million, of whom about 30,000 still lived in the medina (old city): a teeming medieval town, to some minds the largest living museum in the world. Here Yemen's fairy-tale architecture finds its fullest expression in tower houses of brick and clay, decorated like wedding cakes with casements, gables and white friezes frizzy with squiggles and squirls. By night, the medina glows gently through scores of fretted *takhrim* windows, through milky alabaster or tiny glass panes of every colour.

It is a masterpiece without plan or plumb line, the organic growth of 2000 years' habitation. In the medina's tangled depths there are more than 30 *caravanserais* – merchants' inns now used as warehouses – and 40 souks connected to alleys devoted to countless different crafts. Camels harnessed to giant pestles in dark stalls grind oil presses; in the fiery Souk al-Haddadin, smiths sing to the rhythmic beat of their hammers, and pungent white smoke puffs from the Souk al-Qasib, where the *mada'a* (hubble-bubble) makers are piecing together their mysterious contraptions. In the Souk al-Shanabi, apprentices of several crafts combine to fashion the curved *jambiya* daggers, the symbol of Yemeni manhood. There are veilmakers, bookbinders, brass-beaters and Koran-sellers; there is also a silver market, where lamps and antique weapons are also sold, and the best spice market in all Yemen. The great mosque in the medina was laid out on the instructions of the Prophet himself; some of

Craft such as this once rode the monsoons to India and back. Now they are relegated to coastal trade – or to smuggling whisky across the straits from Africa.

All hands to the sayf al-bahr *(sword of the sea) as a fishing boat is launched. Yemeni seafarers have ranged every coast from Africa to China.*

Fish makes up an important part of the Yemeni diet. As well as being consumed fresh, various species are salted for sale deep in the Arabian interior.

Yemeni weddings involve at least three days of ritual and celebrations – all strictly segregated. The women's finery testifies to the social cohesion of this community in the lowlands of north Yemen. The heavy display of silver jewellery is typical of Yemen, which was famous for its Jewish silversmiths, until most emigrated to Israel. Note the number of bulging cheeks, the tell-tale sign of qat being chewed.

All but submerged in supplies of qat, male wedding guests relax after the wedding feast, for which several sheep were slaughtered. They will pass incense from hand to hand as a blessing, hear pious recitations, and perhaps join in songs to a lute and hand-drum accompaniment.

its columns come from the Christian cathedral that the Ethiopian King Abraha built here 1500 years ago, of which no other trace remains. In all this crush are large vegetable gardens, and even flocks of sheep and goats.

Picturesque – but increasingly impractical – was the message of the 1970s, when the alleys became race tracks for honking cars, trucks and motorbikes. All this was booty brought back by Yemenis employed in the oil industry in Saudi Arabia and the Gulf states. Thoroughfares that were no more than earthen ditches, tramped down by centuries of donkey and mule traffic, and flushed by the irregular downpours, became cratered wadis, filled with soft-drink cans and other modern garbage, raising clouds of dust to meet a drifting smog from new cement factories.

Old Yemen had been biodegradable, with everything recycled naturally. Toilets dribble-dried down the high outside walls, under the purifying rays of the hot sun, while solid waste was stored in a small excrement chamber on the ground floor, to be burned as fuel, and the ash used as fertiliser. In Shibam back in Hadramawt, for example, most homes had piped water by the 1960s, and women no longer had to trudge to the well with goatskins, but this blessing of running water proved a curse, for Shibam lacked sewers. Waste water built up, foundations weakened, and 14 houses had collapsed by the mid-1980s. Similar things happened in San'a and other places. In another town, Ta'iz, in the southern mountains, an outbreak of cholera was traced to raw sewage seeping into drinking wells.

The United Nations Educational, Scientific and Cultural Organization (UNESCO) stepped in to declare San'a and Shibam a unique part of human heritage, and a rescue campaign was begun. The Old City of San'a has had some of its *caravanserais* restored, streets paved and sewers installed, but the deeper problems of preservation in the face of modern expectations and desires – for car parks, supermarkets and fewer stairs to climb – make the future uncertain.

The Yemeni's home is his castle

Old San'a could be a metaphor for the entire Yemen, so suddenly opened up to new prospects and problems. A weak government and a population widely dispersed across a rugged landscape in which communications were difficult – these were just a few of the snags. Not to mention the special factor of the Yemenis themselves: holding to the same desert creed as other Arabians, but here crushed into narrow confines by their mountains, they are dogged individualists, short in stature but high on self-esteem.

They number perhaps 12 million, most living in small villages where the vital statistics stay stubbornly medieval: life expectancy hovers around 50; there are a high birth and infant mortality rates, and female illiteracy runs at well over 90 per cent. The traditional escape has been by migration – Java, New York and Cardiff are just three places where Yemeni communities can be found. But the Gulf oil boom galvanised the process, so that at least a third of the male population has worked abroad at some time, creating an inflationary remittance economy and altering aspirations. Sooner or later, the migrant worker is always drawn home, but he is unlikely to wish to go back to tilling the land; far better to buy a little truck, and call himself a businessman.

Belief in a common origin, distinct from that of the north Arabians, or Adnani, is what binds Yemenis together, and – Aden and the south-west apart – the majority Qahtani (south Arabians) are still integrated into a tribal network predating Islam and adhering to the rigorous family-honour code inherited from the Bedouin. The northern tribes are all the more territorial for being settled and contained; their sheikhs are jealous of their autonomy, and dispense justice according to the unwritten, time-honoured tribal tradition, which takes precedence over Islamic law. The two largest tribal groups or confederations, the Hashid and the Bakil, were long known as the 'wings of the Imamate'. They were the Azidi Imams' most loyal supporters, linked by a common Qahtani heritage and allegiance to the Zaidi form of Shiism, and fiercely scornful of the mostly Sunni townspeople of the coastal regions; it was the loss of Hashid support when the Imam Ahmed had the confederation's paramount sheikh executed in 1959 that in large measure spelled the end of the Imamate. At the same time, the Hashid and Bakil, though tied by blood and alliance, are fierce rivals with one another. They have been fighting each other since before the time of Muhammad and brought North Yemen back to the brink of civil war in 1974; it took mediation by Saudi Arabia to arrange a truce.

Her hair coiffured and make-up applied by a specialist, the bride prepares for the biggest moment of her life. She was not present at the actual ceremony, which was conducted by a qadi *(Islamic lawyer) in the presence of her father and the groom, whom she knows all about but has never met. She did, however, have the right of refusal, and retains a substantial dower in the event of the marriage failing.*

The Hashid can mobilise tens of thousands of armed men at an instant. Their territory is the mountains north of San'a, where they raise stock and cultivate small terraced plots. Hashid men are proud of their moustaches and beards, and until recently grew their hair long. The skirt-like national garment, the *futah,* is held in place by a leather belt in which the *jambiya* is thrust, and across his chest he wears a cartridge belt. A man is not properly dressed without his rifle: he will even wear it at his wedding. The fine-featured Hashid women cover their long hair with a scarf held by a metal or cloth headband, and wear a long robe over baggy trousers. They are not veiled, and are often to be seen working the fields alone, harder workers than the men. Hashid clans live in clusters of multistorey houses backed on to the mountainside; each is home to several generations, the ultimate expression of family cohesion and prestige.

This rubta *(bunch) of qat is enough for a chewing session lasting all afternoon. Heavy users may chew half a dozen* rubtas *a day and spend half their income on Yemen's national drug. Qat is outlawed in the rest of Arabia.*

Whatever its construction, of stone, brick or mud, the plan of the mountain or *wadi* home is vertical, and the steps steep – defiantly so, considering the diminutive size of many Yemenis. Thick walls help to even out big temperature swings between day and night, and windows are of a size to limit summer glare yet allow in the warming rays of winter. The ground floor of a typical tower house accommodates a stable and granary; the first floor is for storage, and above this is found the *diwan,* or reception room; the family floors follow, each with its *al-ma* (water room) consisting of washroom and toilet. Men and women usually sleep in separate rooms, however close their relationship. The kitchen, which has a well shaft down to the ground, is somewhere in this section; the cylindrical *tannur* oven is set into the masonry. The top floor has the *mafraj,* the 'room with a view', the largest and best-appointed room in the house. A roof terrace is also usual.

Life revolves around family and home. The day starts early, the call to *al fajr*, dawn prayer, coming when it is still dark and frigid in the mountain winters. The men go to the mosque, the focus of community life, where problems can be ironed out after prayers. The home is the women's domain; here they wear their colourful long dresses over baggy trousers; should a stranger call, the semitransparent *lithma* is slipped over the face just below the eyes. Housework and cooking are communal tasks accompanied by constant chatter and blaring music from a radio. Bread will be baked more than once in the day, since the Yemenis love it hot.

The whole family gets together for the main meal after *az zuhr*, the midday prayer, unless the men have visitors, in which case they eat first with their guests. *Shafut* is a spicy sour milk concoction, cold and

refreshing, and is often followed by *bint as sahn* (literally, 'girl on a plate'), a crepe-like pastry soaked in honey. The main dish might be *selta,* a sizzling, highly spiced stew that contains lamb or chicken, beans, lentils or anything else handy, served on rice or scooped up with bread. *Hulba* (fenugreek and leek soup) is another favourite. In the south, fish dishes are common. Tea or *qishr* follows the meal, and soon comes the call to *al asr*, afternoon prayer, when the suns drops to an angle of 45° to the earth.

Then, about this time, everything stops for qat.

What is qat?

According to the British Bank of the Middle East, in its advice to businessmen:

'A habit peculiar to the Yemenis is the chewing of a mildly narcotic leaf called *qat,* mainly throughout the afternoon. Parties are held at which much business may be settled, and a foreigner honoured with an invitation should accept...addiction to the taste need not be feared.'

Qat (Catha edulis) is an evergreen bush that thrives in the mountains above 3000 feet. The shiny leaf contains complex chemical compounds, including a stimulant closely related to the 'upper' amphetamine. It is the last of Yemen's bounty, some dubious consolation for the lost prosperity of frankincense, myrrh and coffee. Sufi mystics would sometimes munch it in their quest for divine insight, and in recent times it has become central to Yemeni life. Taxi drivers swear by it; it is said to lighten all hard or monotonous work and to stimulate the intellect, but most of all, it is cause for the major Yemeni social activity, the afternoon qat party in the *mafraj.* For hours on end, a host and his cronies will cram leaf after leaf into their mouths, working them into solid green balls of cud that bulge out the cheeks. The group typically passes through an animated phase, then gradually becomes quiet and ruminative.

Women have their own afternoon gatherings – *tafrita* – but never at the same time or in the same house as the

Weekly village markets like this one south of Ta'izz are an important feature of Yemeni life. They number more than 500, and some date back hundreds of years.

men. For such expeditions, they usually cloak themselves in the black *sharshaf,* or the equally enveloping but colourful *sitara,* which they cast off in the sanctuary of their hostess's home. The *tafrita* is an unrestrained sister to the English tea party, at which gossip and the most intimate details of private life are avidly shared over *qat.*

Qat apologists see it as a harmless habit that brings Yemenis together in good-hearted camaraderie. Critics see it as wrecking the country's economy and health. Increasingly, slopes once covered with coffee have been turned over to qat, which is worthless as an export, yet five times more profitable than any other crop on the domestic market. Time-consuming as well as expensive, qat chewing may take up to four hours a day and up to half the family income. As a hunger suppressant, it may contribute to the malnourishment of the poor by inducing them to cut down on their already meagre diet of bread and overcooked vegetables.

Foreigners have often been enthusiastic. 'I quickly became accustomed to using qat, and derived great pleasure from its gentle stimulation and the vivid dream which followed,' a 19th-century French traveller wrote. As for Islamic scholars, they have wrestled with the moral issue of *qat* for centuries – as with that of alcohol, coffee, tobacco and other such substances. Failing to find a clear directive in the Koran, they ruled the plant 'doubtful'. This ruling has yielded different results in different places. Puritanical Saudi Arabia has no doubts and bans it outright, as do the Gulf states. But not even the Communists managed to wean the Yemenis away from their obsession, though they did try to restrict its use in the south to the weekends.

There are added complications. One tricky one is that *qat* is said to cause an ill-matched loss of sexual drive in men, on the one hand, but an increase in sexual drive in women, on the other. Whatever the truth of that, it certainly causes constipation and tends to leave the user feeling restive. This compounds the difficulties. One recommended route to a good night's sleep is a shot of whisky, but this is definitely not proscribed by Islam. Fortunately the Yemenis have an understanding of God's capacity for forgiveness. By the late 1980s, the old coffee port of Mocha had acquired a new claim to fame as the unofficial headquarters of whisky smuggling.

In fact, this flexibility may perhaps be seen as a surprising and indirect tribute to the Zaidi form of Islam, which has always been comparatively relaxed about the outward observances of religion – it does not, for example, insist absolutely on the need to pray five times a day – whilst still maintaining a proud spiritual tradition. It is attitudes such as these, as well as Yemen's rugged landscape, that have helped to make it what it is: one of the most distinctive and appealing of Arab countries.

Yemeni dress styles vary greatly between regions, and even from town to town. This family party is wearing a type of sitara *popular in San'a. A hundred miles away, the women of Rada' favour much lighter patterns.* Sitaras *are made of cloth imported from India; they are worn with brightly decorated veils of black muslin.*

Iraq

Two of the most renowned rivers of antiquity make their way across Iraq. The Tigris and Euphrates create stretches of fertility in a desert landscape, blending eventually into the marshes of the south. Together they have helped to shape a country of mosaics: mosaics of different landscapes, of different civilisations and cultures, of different religions and peoples. In recent times Iraq has become known for the tyranny of Saddam Hussein, but not even he has been able to destroy his country's many faces – the Iraq of the Marsh Arabs, the Iraq of Baghdad and the holy cities of Shiite Islam, the pastoral Iraq lying between the two great rivers, desert Iraq, and the Iraq of the Kurds and Christians.

An immense swamp created by the merging Tigris and Euphrates rivers is home to the Marsh Arabs, who have adapted the customs of the desert to their watery world. This typical settlement rides on artificial islands of layered mud and reeds.

Previous page:
Expressing pride as much as grief, this memorial in Baghdad commemorates Iraqi soldiers killed in the war with Iran – and for good measure celebrates a victory over the same enemy more than 1300 years earlier. The design is a striking marriage of traditional and modern.

Along with their domestic chores, marsh wives share in the work of their husbands, starting with reed gathering.

The Land Between the Rivers

Where the great rivers Tigris and Euphrates meet before entering the Persian Gulf is the site of the Garden of Eden, or so legend has it. With more certainty it can be proved that through subsequent ages the reed-choked marshes in the cleft of the rivers have served as a sanctuary. The British Museum has a bas-relief showing the Assyrian King Sennacherib vainly hunting fugitives here. Everything depicted is familiar today – the canoes, water buffalo, dumpy reed houses, people skulking in the reeds – yet the sculpture is 2700 years old.

Even the warrior nation of Assyria at the height of its power might have been awed by recent events taking place in its operational area. For much of the 1980s the eastern flank of the marshes was the front line in the Iran-Iraq war, the latest re-enactment of an ancient Persian-Arab blood feud in which the Iranians made up in fervour what they lacked in heavy armour, and suicidal waves of child conscripts cleared minefields with their bodies and stormed tank formations. The Iraqis replied with poison gas. The death toll touched a million before a halt was called, with no net gains of ground by either side. That war was scarcely over before another flared: the Gulf War. The skies now became filled with incoming missiles and warplanes, dispatched to drive the Iraqi occupiers out of Kuwait. The region where, in the Biblical account, mankind began, found itself repeatedly becoming a cockpit of war.

A precarious plenty

Al-Dijlis and Al-Furat, the Tigris and the Euphrates, spring from the same Anatolian mountains, and for more than 1000 miles they play tag in roughly the same south-westerly direction, tracing two green furrows through the desert before becoming one in the Shatt al Arab, the 'river of the Arabs'. They bear the life force of water impregnated with rich silt, but sometimes the water arrives in too great abundance, for in springtime the rivers are charged with the snow-melt of Anatolia. Occasional devastating floods have wiped out entire peoples. The mother of all floods, the Biblical flood, was surely one of those. In recent years, there has been an opposite problem as well: dams in south-eastern Turkey have affected the water flow in certain seasons of the year of the great rivers as they pass through Syria and Iraq. Both nations have protested at this infringement of their ancient rights.

Mesopotamia – the 'land between the rivers' that forms the heart of modern Iraq – is one of the cradles of Western civilisation. Before even Old Testament times, the precarious plenty of the Tigris-Euphrates basin provided just the right combination of challenge and opportunity to stimulate the earliest herders and farmers into extraordinary creative endeavours. Sumer is the ancient name for southern Mesopotamia, where one of the first urban civilisations arose in the area between present-day Basra and Baghdad more than 5000 years ago. Possibly the most innovative people who ever lived, the Sumerians invented irrigation, cereal cultivation, the wheel, mathematics, astronomy, and literature. They created the first known written language, using a snapped-off marsh reed to make impressions on tablets made from river clay. The number 60, sacred to the god An, was their basic unit of calculation: hence our 60-minute hour and the 360 degrees of the circle, both Sumerian concepts.

With their spider's web of canals feeding gardens of date palms, it must have seemed at some early moment in time that the Sumerians had created a kind of paradise. Unfortunately, achievement always has its dark side, and like Cain and Abel, war and civilisation grew up together here. Sumer fell and Babylon rose. In 728 BC the terrible Assyrians, with fast chariots and weapons of iron, razed Babylon to the ground. They in

The jabbayah *(headcloth) wrapped tight as protection both from the sun and mosquitoes, also protects against cold winter nights on the marshes.*

The mashuf *is the gondola of the swamps, as practical as it is picturesque. Highly manoeuvrable and of shallow draft, it has not changed in thousands of years.*

The design of this typical reed mudhif *(guesthouse) has not changed since the dawn of history. Such structures may have inspired Classical architecture, making the cathedral-like effect less of a coincidence.*

turn, slaked by conquest, were overthrown by the Medes. In 606 BC the mighty Assyrian city of Nineveh was stormed and 'became a desolation, a place for beasts to lie down in', in the words of the Jewish prophet Zephaniah. Babylon rose again under the Chaldeans of Nebuchadnezzar, who destroyed Jerusalem and built the Hanging Gardens, wonder of the age, until Cyrus the Great of Persia tumbled them down. After Cyrus the Great came Alexander the Great. Persians, Greeks, Seleucids, Parthians, Romans and Persians again all came to conquer the land between the rivers and maintain the cycle of sack and renewal.

In AD 634, an Arab force under Khalid bin Walid, 'the Sword of Islam', stormed out of the desert and conquered all before them for a new faith. They built a new capital, Baghdad, and fostered a new golden age. But it was not to last. In 1258, Mongol hoards laid to waste the city of the Arabian nights, and a century later they did it again. This time there was no renewal. Irrigation systems collapsed, the precious waters dispersed into swamps, gardens reverted to the desert, and nomads from beyond the Euphrates grazed their

herds over mounds that had once been the palaces of kings.

Centuries of stagnation as a distant tributary of the Ottoman Empire came to an end in 1917, when British forces seized Mesopotamia in the course of the desert campaign against the Turks – made famous by the deeds of T.E. Lawrence (of Arabia) leading Arab forces in a daring guerrilla offensive. Modern Iraq was created out of three Ottoman provinces, with a British-installed monarchy that was swept away in 1958 in a surge of new-found nationalism. Out of this confusion a man was to emerge who identified himself with Nebuchadnezzar and who had visions of creating a new Babylon. His name was Saddam Hussein.

The marshes of Eden

According to the Sumerian account of the Creation, the god Enlil (Marduk to the Babylonians) 'built a reed platform upon the surface of the waters, and created dust and poured it around the platform', and thereby created the world. The procedure is followed to this day in the course of home construction on the grey-green delta marshes of southern Iraq, where a way of life pre-dating the Flood endured unchanged into modern times, secure behind its reed curtain from the rise and fall of dynasties.

The marshes are as extensive as they are incongruous in the arid Middle East, more than 6000 square miles of reed beds and lagoons stretching from just beyond Basra in the south to within 200 miles of Baghdad in the north, spilling into Iran in the east and poking a wet tentacle at the parched emptiness of Arabia to the west. First impressions are bewitching; the palette of colours and lights, the subtle sounds and the silences make it seem a dream world. It is also a daunting one. The summer marsh is a steam furnace, with temperatures topping 50°C (122°F) in the shade of the towering qasab reeds. Winter brings chill, misty dawns, and cold winds that whine down the waterways. Sudden icy gales and squalls crash down from the mountains of Kurdistan, sending the reeds reeling and capsizing boats. Occasional hailstorms can kill. The entire aquatic universe is never still, but bobbing up and down at the whim of the great rivers' flow. Not surprisingly, the

Marsh reeds are split, pounded and woven into mats that are shipped in bulk and used throughout Iraq. An 8 foot by 4 foot mat with a herringbone pattern takes about two hours to make.

marshes have their legendary beasts and magic places – hairy monsters like the mythical Afa and Anfish, and Hufaidh, the island that no man may look upon and keep his senses.

The Madan, as the Marsh Arabs call themselves, were hardly known to the outside world until the 1950s, when Wilfred Thesiger left the desert to live and write among them. He found a self-contained universe unchanged in 5000 years, even to the design of reed homesteads and the high-prowed, needle-slim *mashuf* canoe. The Madan culture is tribal Bedouin, the codes and manners of the desert adapted to life at the opposite extreme, but the faces reveal a far wider heritage, from the round faces of the old Sumerians to the high cheekbone of the Mongol. Fair hair is not uncommon, and there are green and blue eyes among the brown. The young girls are often strikingly beautiful.

The villages lie in clearings in the reeds. To create a new homestead, an area of water large enough for house and yard is enclosed with a very high reed fence. The interior is packed with reeds and rushes until the stack rises above the surface of the water. The containing fence is broken inwards to lie across the stack, which is piled with more rushes and trampled down until a satisfactory foundation has been created. For a more durable foundation, a layer of scooped-up mud is inserted. Bundles of qasab reeds (thick as a middle finger and up to 25 feet tall) are driven into this base, each bundle securely bound along its length so that it becomes a stout pillar, which forms an arch when bent over. A line of arches forms the frame of the marsh house, reed-beamed and buttressed, roofed with reed matting, and sided with reed lattice. Should the platform sink, or the water level rise, the owner has only to lay down more reeds and rushes. Years of layering creates a permanent island.

Each island is a miniature farmyard, its load of buffalo, cows, sheep, fowl, cats and rowdy dogs turning the soggy platform into an overloaded ark. The water buffalo are the lords of the marshes. A family will usually own about half a dozen of the ponderous black beasts, and pamper them like babies; at night a cow and calf will sometimes muzzle right into the house. In the morning, the buffalo are shooed off the platform with a mighty splosh, to spend their days nostril-deep in the cooling water, munching placidly until drawn home by the prospect of juicy sedges that have been gathered for them. In winter, if conditions are too chilly for their liking, they stay put on the platform while the family does all their foraging. The reward is a copious supply of rich milk, and dung for fuel.

Lions once infested the fringes of the marshes. Sir Henry Layard, the 19th-century excavator of Nineveh, observed regular lion hunts around the reed banks, and until quite recent times there were people who could remember grunts and guttural roars carrying across the marshes at night. The scourge now is the wild pig.

The marsh oven is usually sited outdoors, sometimes on its own islet 'moored' beside the house – a protection against the risk of fire.

The men of the marshes (right) gather by night to drink bitter coffee brewed in brass pots, to settle disputes and discuss marriage arrangements. The coffee hearth is located at the centre of the mudhif. *Procedures are otherwise identical to those of the desert Bedouin.*

Viewed from inside, the mudhif *reveals its clever construction. The arches are bundles of giant reeds bent double and tightly trussed.*

The marshes teem with fish, especially various species of carp and barbel. Tastiest is the binni, *which is split, then spitted on a reed splinter and cooked over a fire. Known as* masguf, *this dish is very popular in Baghdad.*

These crash through the shallows in large packs, and grow enormous and dangerous: 300 pounds or more, with a lethal bite, and razor-sharp tusks. Many Madan bear the scars of encounters with pigs.

The tilting casements of Old Basra suffered like the rest of the city from massive bombardment during the war with Iran, when half the population fled. Recovery had just begun when Basra suffered renewed attack during the Gulf War, and then a civil uprising.

The Madan themselves are the other danger. Tribes adhere to the sensitive honour code of the desert, and it takes little to trigger a blood feud, or for it to get out of hand, especially since war has speeded up the acquisition of automatic weapons. The rules of blood feuding are arcane. *Fasl* (compensation to settle the debt of honour) may take the form of buffalo and money, as well as *talawi,* girls of marriageable age.

Marsh women live contradictory lives: segregated, they nevertheless enjoy great freedom. They do not intrude into the male fastness of the *mudhif* (guesthouse), and they are shy before strangers, but not in their own home, or among neighbours, and their influence grows with age. They do the cooking and share in much of the work, punting canoes to market, collecting reeds, bringing fodder to the buffalo, although they may not milk them. As with the camels of the desert Bedouin, milking is a man's task.

From about the age of six, boys and girls have their own tiny canoes, and are trusted to venture forth to cut reeds or keep an eye on the buffalo. The girls marry young, 14 to 16; the boys somewhat older. Weddings are long, loud and joyful; guests gathering at the groom's village in full finery, the men armed to the teeth, the women glinting and clinking with anklets, bracelets and silver head ornaments. They then proceed in convoy to the home of the bride, where the tribal standard is raised and celebrations last all day, with much firing into the air. The men dance the *hoca,* a rhythmic circular stomp that also serves as a tune-up for battle, and the women cry out enthusiastic support.

Later everyone takes to the boats again, bringing back the demure bride, who travels with her possessions piled into a big *mashhuf,* some of them newly purchased out of the bride price the head of her family has received. The men then adjourn to the *mudhif* for a rousing party, with songs and solo dancing to the accompaniment of hand-drums. Around midnight, a ribald chorus of jokes marks the groom's departure to join his bride, and the village settles down to wait, suspensefully. Some time later, a single rifle shot breaks the tension, and the hubbub and singing breaks out anew: it is the groom signalling a successful consummation.

During the 1970s, marsh life began to change

dramatically. Government intrusion brought with it agricultural co-operatives, clinics and schools, and there were heady plans to restore the region to its ancient Sumerian glory with the construction of dams and irrigation systems. Then came two murderous wars, and the marshes became the haunt of bands of deserters and anti-Saddam rebels, and of thousands in flight from Basra and other cities. The long-term future of the Madan is still anyone's guess.

Venice of the East

Basra was the home port of Sinbad the Sailor, 'a towne of great trade of spices and drugges', an admiring Elizabethan voyager noted. It is 60 miles up the Shatt al Arab, the spout down which the coffee-brown waters of the Tigris and Euphrates pour into the Arabian Gulf.

Founded in AD 637 by the conquering Arabs, Basra became a glittering emporium on the East-West trade route – the Venice of the East, as enthusiasts liked to proclaim it – and there are enchanting descriptions of grand houses, pomegranate gardens and date glades reflecting in its tangle of canals. 'The Hollanders bring spices every year. The English carry pepper and some cloves', a French nobleman wrote in the 1630s. 'There are merchants from Constantinople, Smyrna, Aleppo, Damascus, Cairo and other parts of Turkie . . . from Moussul, Baghdad, Mesopotamia, Assyria.'

Glimpses of an older Basra, which still give some idea of its former wealth and glory, now survive chiefly in its Ashar quarter. Here, city-dwellers, visiting Marsh Arabs and prosperous farmers from the fertile lands between the rivers to the north mingle in a happy confusion. Enticing smells of coffee and numerous herbs and spices hang heavily in the narrow streets and alleys of the bazaar area, while stallholders and street-

Carpets are made using techniques that are hundreds of years old. Here, one finished product is being carefully washed – the last stage before it is sent to the market to be sold.

This woman from Al Qush is an Assyrian member of a Christian sect that separated from the Byzantine Church 200 years before the dawn of Islam. Iraq's ethnic and religious diversity make it a difficult country to govern.

A martyr's tomb in Karbala (right) attracts a constant flow of pilgrims. Shia Muslims rank Karbala next to nearby Najaf in holiness, and consider the combined pilgrimage to be the spiritual equivalent of the journey to Mecca. Before the war, Iranians came here in great numbers.

In October 680, Hussein, the son of Ali and grandson of the Prophet Muhammad, was killed with members of his family near the site of this martyrs' mosque in Karbala. In March 1991, Islam's oldest, deepest feud flared into bitter fighting around Hussein's tomb.

sellers cry their various wares – including most things from vegetables to electronic games. Near by, a canal leading off the Shatt al Arab is lined with the beautiful, yellow-brick mansions built by Basra's 19th-century merchant elite, now sadly crumbling. Enclosed wooden balconies, known as *shenasils,* many of them carved, others painted shades of blue and green, overhang the canal, allowing those inside to watch the activities of the outside world. Many are protected from the worst of the summer glare and heat by broad wooden awnings, propped up over the windows.

But Basra lives off more than memories. It is Iraq's second-largest city after Baghdad and its chief port. It is also the centre of an important date-growing area. Iraq is famous for its dates – indeed, it is the world's largest exporter of them – and for hundreds of years the best groves were those that lined the Shatt al Arab. Dates are a staple of the local diet, and much more besides, being used to make sugar, alcohol, vinegar and cattle feed. Even the stones find a use as fuel. The distinctive taste of chicken cooked over a date-stone fire bears witness to the qualities of this remarkable fruit.

In the early 1960s, more than 30 million date palms graced the Shatt al Arab, shaking their fronds at every slight breeze and providing a habitat for exotic birdlife. By midway through the war with Iran – which lies on the far bank – at least 60 per cent of the groves were gone. Basra fared as badly, a sitting duck for the heavy artillery that pounded it relentlessly. A shambles when the cease-fire took hold in 1988, the city was made the focus of post-war reconstruction efforts. Canals were dredged, new roads constructed, entire districts rebuilt. All this was nullified by the Gulf War. Allied bombardment early in 1991 was followed by bloody civil insurrection after Iraq's ignominious defeat. In a destructive orgy, anything still standing and associated with the authorities was torched. The regime then turned its tanks on the populace, exacting collective punishment.

In the desperate months of deprivation that followed, ancient beliefs were revived, now stronger than ever. Some mothers dressed baby sons as girls, to protect them from the 'evil eye' of others jealous from having lost their own infants, and believers who had made the Muslim pilgrimages found themselves being touched and clutched by the weak and diseased, desperate for a lifeline to God.

Partisans of Ali

The trail of destruction led up the Euphrates to engulf Iraq's holy cities, Najaf and Karbala. It was along this same route, 1300 years ago, that the Sunni-Shia schism slashed like a scimitar through Islam, creating a division as deep as that between Catholic and Protestant in Christendom. Shia is short for Shiat Ali, the Party of Ali, the Prophet Muhammad's virtuous cousin and son-in-law – and spiritual heir, according to the Shia. Other

Muslims, who became known as Sunni, or orthodox, looked outside the Prophet's family to the aristocracy of Mecca, Islam's birthplace, for the choice of caliph (successor). Rivalry led to warfare, and for the first time, just outside Basra, Muslim fought Muslim.

Ali won the battle, but was then murdered. A generation later, Ali's son Hussein, grandson of the Prophet, was invited to lead a revolt, only to be betrayed. Bravely, on October 10, 680, Hussein, his family, and a little band of loyal retainers faced the Caliph Yezid's forces on the banks of the Euphrates, and were annihilated. This dramatic martyrdom of the Prophet's descendants transformed a political faction into a religious movement charged with potent notions of sacrifice, the effects of which are felt throughout the Middle East to this day. The Shia regard themselves as the opposition in Islam, opponents of privilege and power, and Hussein remains a compelling role model for young zealots.

Hussein was buried on the plains of Karbala where he fell. Soon men began to visit the spot to pray, and a town arose, with a mosque to house the martyr's remains. The holy city of Najaf likewise grew up in the desert around Ali's tomb, over which the faithful built a great mosque with golden domes to the man they proclaimed 'The Saint of God'. Pilgrims usually approach the shrine on their knees, kissing the sill of the threshold, and then, with palms raised, recite the opening *surah* (chapter) of the Koran, al Fateha. The tomb lies under a dome decorated with blue emeralds, surrounded by a silver fence. To a ceaseless buzz of prayer, pilgrims circle it twice, kiss the fence, and rub objects against it, often a scarf, which can be cut up and shared among friends back home while others throw coins or jewellery inside the fence, hoping for some boon.

Karbala and Najaf are 50 miles apart, and to many Shia the dual pilgrimage matches in merit the pilgrimage to Mecca. Better still is to be buried here, as near as possible to Ali's tomb. Coffins flow in from all corners of the Shia world, draped in green and strapped on to car roofs for the drive from Basra, or shipped up the Euphrates in the holds of the big *mahailas* (sailing barges). The necropolis of Najaf, Wadi as-Salaam (River of Peace), is unique of its kind: it takes up half the city, a rolling sea of headstones.

The distinction between Shia and Sunni has bedevilled modern Iraq just as it did early Islam. Southern Iraq is Shia Muslim, while northern Iraq is Sunni Muslim. The Sunni wield political power, even though they are in the minority; the Shia are generally

Big red British double-deckers rumbling across the Tigris lend a touch of London to Baghdad. British troops captured the city from the Turks in 1917, and a British-imposed political system survived in Iraq until 1958. The Shuhada Bridge is one of a dozen city bridges. Several were bombed during the Gulf War.

poorer. Iraq's neighbour and rival, Iran, is the only Islamic country in which the Shia dominate numerically, culturally and politically, and so Iraq's Shia might be expected to look to their Iranian counterparts for leadership and support. But the most powerful group in Iran's population are Persians – traditional foes of the Arabs. As long as Iran was the enemy, Iraq's Shia rank-and-file stayed loyal, deaf to strident Iranian appeals to their religious sensibilities. But when that war was over, only to be followed by the fiasco of the Kuwait invasion, the partisans of Ali rose as of old.

The fighting was particularly fierce in the holy cities. The centre of Karbala was reduced to rubble, its golden domes blasted by shellfire. Shia die-hards made a last stand in the holiest mosques, and army rockets and artillery pulverised vivid blue walls decorated with intricate inscriptions from the Koran. When it was over, Najaf had a fresh harvest of martyrs.

The new Babylon

'You are the perfume of Iraq, oh Saddam,
The water of the two rivers, oh Saddam,
The sword and the shield, oh Saddam.'

The fulsome praises crooned over Iraqi radio in recent times echo the hyperbolic style of the desert praise-maker before his sheikh. The Iranians went into battle with images of Ali, the Shia saint, emblazoned on their tanks. The Iraqis trusted in posters of their jowly, mustachioed president, Saddam Hussein, a most secular messiah.

The modern history of Iraq reads like Macbeth, only bloodier. There were 23 coups or attempted coups between the ousting of the Turks and the coming to power of Saddam, strongman of the Ba'ath (Arab Socialist Resurrection) Party. Few organisations in the world are so harshly disciplined as the Ba'ath, and few operate so secretly, yet in the manner in which it has been dominated by one family – Saddam's, from a town on the upper Tigris called Tikrit – it could not be more traditional. Kinship groups with deeply ingrained family or tribal loyalties make up the ill-fitting mosaic that is Iraq; Saddam (the name translates as 'the one who confronts') set out to hammer these groups into a modern, powerful nation-state at whatever cost to individual liberty. To his credit, large sums were spent on improving the lives of ordinary people. Villages were electrified and schools and hospitals dot the wilderness. He also rebuilt Baghdad.

Despite the government's enthusiasm for large Western-style shopping centres, Baghdad still offers the traditional delights of souk browsing and bargaining over a proffered cup of tea or coffee.

The souks resound to the clang of hammers tapping out water pitchers, coffeepots, kettles, giant platters – to say nothing of wall plaques adorned with the smiling countenance of Saddam Hussein. The products of tinsmith and coppersmith go on sale next to mass-produced plastic and aluminium utensils.

Baghdad! Only in the name does modern Baghdad retain the magic of its old image as the city of the Arabian Nights. It is more than 1200 years since the Caliph al-Mansur consulted his astrologer, then set 100,000 workmen to build Madinat al-Salaam ('The City of Peace'), with its perfectly circular walls two miles across, on a bank of the Tigris where the main trade routes crossed. Here, at the glittering court of caliphs who proclaimed themselves the 'Shadow of God on Earth' (and who underlined the point by keeping an executioner with drawn sword by their side at all times), the character of early Islam was reshaped by the brilliant cultural infusion of the conquered Persians.

By the 9th century, in the reign of the great patron of the arts, Haroun al-Raschid, Baghdad (somehow City of Peace never caught on) was a fabulous metropolis, the richest and most learned place on earth, a magnet for the most accomplished philosophers, scientists, poets and artists. Among the most lasting and famous of their works was the magnificent collection of tales known as *The Thousand and One Nights*, in which the beautiful Scheherazade tells her husband, King Schariar, the stories of Aladdin, Ali Baba, Sinbad the sailor and many others. It is all part of a plan devised by Scheherazade to save her life and that of many other women. For, ever since discovering the infidelity of his first wife the king has vowed to marry a new wife and kill her every day – only his desire to hear the endings of Scheherazade's tales keeps him from continuing with his cruel scheme.

The reign of Haroun al-Raschid was Baghdad's golden age, after which came centuries of decline. It took the oil boom of the 1970s and the grandiose fantasies of a Saddam Hussein to resurrect the city from neglect – though in the process much that had character and crumbly charm was also swept away. Saddam went about the job in much the same manner as the Caliph Mansur. Leading architects from outside – this time from Europe and America – were commissioned to create a capital worthy of a nation aspiring to the leadership of the Arab world. There was a deadline: Baghdad was to have hosted the 1982 conference of non-aligned nations. But the war with Iran was not the walkover Saddam had anticipated, and the meeting was switched elsewhere. Nevertheless, Iraq had a new capital, with a parade of luxury hotels along the Tigris, block after block of housing complexes, a fine new sewage system, new government buildings, monuments, a dozen bridges, a new airport (the Saddam International), and a network of highways twirling round and through the city with so many interchanges that it might be Germany, or Texas – until one comes

Bedouin tent design is standard throughout the Middle East: bands of goat-hair cloth stretched over posts to provide airy shade. Flaps cover the gap on chilly desert nights.

Iraqi peasant homes vary from region to region, but are usually of baked mud and built around a courtyard. Nowadays most sport a television aerial.

These two nomad women were photographed near ancient Ur, from where the Biblical patriarch Abraham set out on his travels. It is tempting to conjure up pictures of Sarah and Hagar, the patriarch's spouses, whose appearance was surely little different, despite a gap of 3500 years.

The pointed bonnet distinguishes girl from boy as they are slung aboard a donkey for a journey across the Syrian desert in western Iraq. Iraqi nomads are shepherds who forsook the camel for the horse and donkey a long time ago. Less then 1 per cent of the population is nomadic, even though much of the country is desert.

What does the future hold for these little Kurdish girls perched on a housetop? About 20 per cent of the Iraqi population are Kurds, a fiercely independent mountain people who have been in constant conflict with the state since its inception.

This timeless scene of horsemen in Kurdistan is deceptively peaceful. Kurdish guerrillas control most of the mountain region and claim the nearby oilfields of Kirkuk which fell within traditional Kurdish territory.

upon a sign announcing 'Babylon 100 kilometres'.

Nebuchadnezzar's Babylon lies south of Baghdad, along a dull road lined with date palms, mud-brick villages and, in recent years, giant portraits of Saddam Hussein. Conquerors and archaeologists have left very little of the great city of antiquity. The dragon-guarded Ishtar Gate is in Berlin, and the shaft of black basalt inscribed with Hammurabi's legal code is in the Louvre in Paris (having first been taken to Iran as war booty in the 12th century BC). As a result, the Iraqis rebuilt part of Babylon – enough to justify a giant joint portrait featuring the skirted Babylonian king with the man who aspired to emulate him. There was a dedication: 'From Nebuchadnezzar to Saddam Hussein.'

Saddam City

Baghdad does not live by the muezzins' call to prayer, but by the clamour of traffic criss-crossing the new arteries of a city which has expanded so fast that its many palm groves have been gobbled up whole. Rural families have flocked into the capital at such a rate that one in every four Iraqis – more than 4 million – is now a Baghdadi. A million are accommodated in Saddam City, a sprawling development of little tawny-brown dwellings where a slum used to be; the people have not had time to forsake old ways, and pack their yards with chickens and goats and lots of bright flowers.

Tahrir Square, on the left bank by the Jumhuriyah Bridge, is the heart of the city, from where the major thoroughfares radiate, all packed with processions of red double-decker buses, ubiquitous mementos of the departed British. There are women about, fashionably dressed, educated, and holding some of the highest offices in the land. There are women engineers, doctors, pilots, architects, lawyers. Overall, women account for a quarter of the Iraqi work force. Ten years of war account in part for this emancipation, extraordinary for an Arab country, but it is also Ba'ath Party doctrine to reject Islamic fundamentalism, with its emphasis on the

The Kurdish peasant cuts a dashing figure – and the image is no deception. Deeply attached to his cultural and tribal roots, he makes a doughty fighter when called upon.

seclusion of women. Men's clubs, on the other hand, are a thriving survivor of the British presence. Men also enjoy the sanctuary of their favourite *chaikhana* (tearoom) to read the newspaper, smoke a narguile, or play backgammon.

Alcohol is legal and so is gambling. There is striptease on Abu Nawas Street, a neon-lit stretch of clubs and bars named after a poet celebrated for his erotic verse. Hundreds of Filipino and Thai bar girls once plied their trade here. Iraqis replaced them, some evidently war widows. The Kuwaitis, barred from drinking at home, were among Abu Nawas Street's best customers, and slightly unsteady figures in white robes were a feature of the scene before the Iraqi invasion.

The Allied bombing of Baghdad during the Gulf War was precise enough to render the city momentarily as useless as a shiny new domestic appliance with its wiring pulled out. In the centre the carcase of the telecommunications centre became an unscheduled monument to disaster; government ministries were badly damaged and bridges were hit, as were the central post office, telephone exchanges, the national palace, and power and water treatment plants. Even though casualties were surprisingly light, people were reduced for a time to drinking from sewage drains.

These Kurdish women selling yoghurt in Sulaimaniyah are Muslim like most Iraqis, but are ethnically and linguistically much closer to the Iranians.

Christians in the crannies

Iraq's torrid dry summer is very slightly relieved by the *shamal,* a bone-dry breeze wafting southwards. At other seasons, the gusty *sharqi* kicks up violent storms that close the airport and clog the capital in fine gritty sand as it is blown back up north.

Mosul, the major city of northern Iraq, used to supply Europe with muslin, whose name is derived from the city. Mosul's main products nowadays are less romantic: oil, sulphur and sulphuric acid. Here was ancient Assyria, and the ruins of Nimrud and Nineveh are not the sole reminders of long ago. There are still some 150,000 Assyrians who adhere to Christian beliefs that were practised in Mesopotamia before Islam. Indeed, the brands of faith practised by Iraq's Christians as a whole reflect the antiquity and diversity of their communities: Chaldeans (Assyrians who give their allegiance to the Pope in Rome); distinctive Syrian Orthodox and Syrian Catholic communities (who speak Aramaic, a language in use centuries before the Arab conquest); as well as groups of Armenian and Greek Orthodox Christians. In the south, there are also intriguing groups of Sabbeans, who claim to be followers of John the Baptist. Until the 19th century at least, they too used Aramaic for writing, though they spoke Arabic – in more recent times, they have produced two of Iraq's most distinguished modern poets: Lemia Abbas Amara and Abdul Razzah Abdul Wahed. Back in the north, the little flocks of Christians

support their own monasteries and gain strength from the richness of their liturgy and communal occasions such as a marriage, when the band plays, incense puffs, ornaments shine, and the bride is resplendent in classic white dress.

Less fortunate are the Yazidis, who live in small, isolated, impoverished groups in the Sinjar Mountains west of Mosul, practising a unique religious fusion of paganism, Zoroastrianism, Christianity and Islam – a heretical mixture that has earned them centuries of persecution. This is chiefly a result of their unusual attitude towards the devil, whom they regard as a fallen angel who will eventually be restored to his place in heaven. God is, of course, good, so they believe that the devil is the one to be propitiated. To this end pilgrims to their most important holy place, Sheikh Adi (named after the founder of their sect), are forbidden to utter the word *Shaitan* (Satan) – all of which has earned them an unwholesome and scarey reputation among other Iraqis as devil worshippers.

The Kurds: 'Those Who Face Death'

East of Mosul, the landscape becomes more rugged, and the problems of the central government more acute. First come the oilfields of Kirkuk – where oil was first struck in Iraq in 1927 – then the wild and beautiful high country of Kurdistan. Terraced villages hug precipitous slopes, their flat-roofed houses climbing one upon

Nimble young fingers and long hours are needed to execute this complicated Kurdish weave. The Kurds' passion for colour and vivid pattern is typified by the girl's dizzy ensemble.

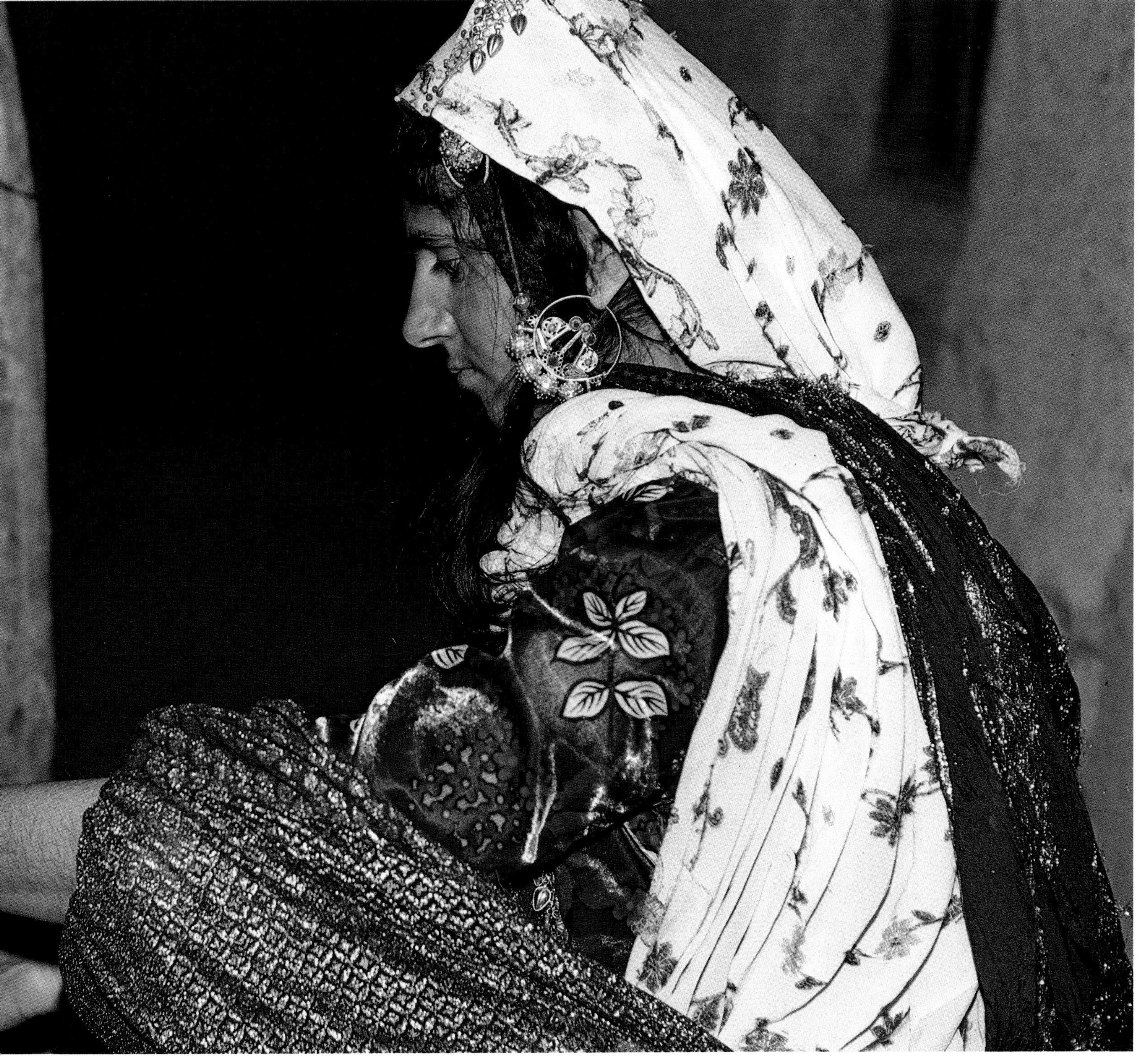

another above streams that tumble through oak forests where bears grub in thickets, up towards high gullies where snowdrifts linger all summer. Herds of mountain goats pick their way across sheer rock faces under the watchful eye of wheeling, hovering vultures – and soldiers with binoculars. For this is disputed territory.

Iraq has more than 4 million Kurds, who are the overwhelming majority in the mountain provinces that form a segment of the Kurdish heartland arching from eastern Turkey and north-west Syria, through former Iranian Azerbaijan to the Zagros Mountains. The Kurds are one of the most ancient surviving peoples of the Middle East, having occupied their mountains probably since prehistoric times. They are mainly Sunni Muslims – they converted to Islam in the 7th century – but like most Iranians they are not Arab, and they speak a sister tongue to the Persian of Iran.

The mountain life is healthy, but hard, particularly on the women, whose work seems never to be done. From sunrise, they are kneading dough, baking bread, milking the animals, making yoghurt and butter, and heaving water from the stream. The mountain diet is wholesome: bread, milk, cheese, yoghurt and vegetables for daily fare; for special occasions, rice wrapped in grape leaves, kebabs, mutton, chicken or goat stews, tomatoes, green beans, onions, okra . . . served in pots that are passed around. The men eat first, then the boys, and only then the women and girls.

The Kurds have a long tradition as warriors. In 401 BC they may well have been the so-called Kardouchoi who attacked a band of 10,000 Greek mercenaries in the service of Cyrus of Persia near the modern town of Kakhu. It was definitely a Kurd, the mighty Saladin, who rallied Islam against the 12th-century Crusaders, and this warrior spirit endures, ready to dare dagger and small arms against jet plane and tank. Kurdish guerrillas, the turbaned and baggy-panted Peshmerga ('Those Who Face Death'), have been locked for decades in an intermittent struggle with the central government – though they have generally been contained since their chief strongholds are in the mountains, well away from the principal centres of the modern Kurdish populations in the cities of the plains. 'Only God and the mountains are on our side', the Kurds say. 'The Kurds have no friends', is another saying.

In springtime, Kurdistan's valleys are cloaked with anemones and blush with tulips. It is also the time when the sap runs strongest in the Peshmerga guerrillas. Gunfire stilled the birdsong in the springs of 1962, 1965, 1974, and throughout the 1980s, when the opportunity presented by the war with Iran was seized. In the spring of 1991, encouraged in the aftermath of Desert Storm to believe that their hour had come, the Peshmerga came down from the mountains and occupied the Kurdish cities, much as the Shia rebels did in the south. Kirkuk was retaken by the Iraqi military, and all the oilfields and milling refugee columns were bombed and strafed by helicopter gunships. But the Peshmerga clung on to the three northern border provinces of Dihok, Arbil and Sulaymaniyah – a 300-mile wedge of the elusive state promised them in 1920 following the dismemberment of the old Ottoman Empire. With the Kurds in the north, the Sunni Muslims in the centre and the Shia in the south, Iraq seemed as fragmented and precarious a unit as ever.

Shrouded women watch the men of Rawanduz dance to celebrate Newroz – New Day – the feast of spring. Fires will burn on the mountaintops and dancing to the zirna *pipe and* dihool *drum will last all night. This town near the Iranian border has a violent history as a focal point of Kurdish nationalism.*

Afghanistan

The Afghans can truly claim to inhabit the crossroads of Asia, with Arabs and Iranians to the west, the Turkic peoples of Uzbekistan to the north, the Chinese to the north-east, and Pakistan and India to the east. Their country came into being in the mid-18th century, under the warrior leadership of Ahmad Shah. This was just one turning point in Afghanistan's history, which has never been tranquil. Greeks, Scythians, Huns, Arabs, Mongols and, most recently, Soviet Russians – all have passed through as invaders. On the other hand, dynasties originating in the territory of modern Afghanistan have also left their mark on neighbouring lands, notably Iran and India.

This scene is typical of the Afghan mountains, where farming often entails a lot of clambering with oxen between crop and distant village for sparse reward. Over-zealous efforts to reform the land tenure system formed one of the causes of the catastrophic civil war.

Previous page:
The Afghan's love of flowers, bright colours and poetry contrasts with his fearsome image, yet it is a natural response to the rigours of life in a hard, arid world. As his beard whitens, so a man's prestige in the community grows, hence the term rish-safid *('white beards') for the village council of elders.*

An Afghan girl learns to 'mother' younger brothers and sisters from a very early age. By the time she is nine or ten, she will have mastered the countless tasks that are expected of a wife.

Crossroads of the World

A dust cloud coils its way up a naked slope, high above the thin green margins of a rocky riverbed. Just beyond one of many hairpin bends, the cloud halts, then dissipates, as it is carried away by the wind. In its place stands a *moutar* – a truck – its overheated engine hissing with menace.

Grudgingly, the driver asks his cargo of male passengers to continue on foot to the top of the pass; the two women riding in the cab may remain. The men jump down with a nonchalance born out of long habit, share a joke, adjust turbans and woollen *patu* blankets slung over their shoulders, then start up the slope with long, purposeful strides that make no concession to the 10,000-foot altitude – one man has a game leg, a war wound, but he will not be bested by the others, and hobbles hard on their heels.

Still protesting, the lightened truck covers the last half-mile to the top, where the driver has to wait only a few minutes for the climbing party to catch up and clamber back on board. Before them stretches a dusty plateau, with a few yellow-ochre crop patches the only signs of man in a pinkish ochre universe. Ochre is the colour of the Afghanistan summer: ochre in an infinite variety of subtle tones and shades; even the sky is ochre from the wind-whisked dust.

In winter, the ochre is overlaid with a uniform coating of snow, until spring rains combine with the snow melt to create short-lived green pastures dancing with poppies and tulips. It is a precarious balance for the people scattered along the high valleys, between the sands and the snows. If there is not enough snow, crops will fail. If the snow melts too quickly, dangerous floods will destroy the crops. Such a flash flood caught the invading army of Alexander the Great 2300 years ago, and persistent drought at the start of the 1970s caused the famine that precipitated the overthrow of Afghanistan's last king.

Harsh, beautiful Afghanistan consists of some 250,000 square miles of mountain and desert stacked around the westernmost spur of the Himalayas: the Hindu Kush –a jagged 600-mile barricade reaching from the Dasht-i-Margo (Desert of Death) in the south to the icy passes of the Pamir Knot, a saw-toothed maze of more than 100 peaks, each one soaring to over 20,000 feet, and reaching into China. Hindu Kush means 'Killer of Hindus', but it was never that discriminating: it permits passage and sanctuary within its folds only to the hardiest. Yet forbidding and isolated as it now seems, this is one of the great crossroads of history, a cultural filter between the Middle East, Central Asia, the Indian subcontinent and even, through the Pamirs, the Far East. This is how Buddhism reached China (and eventually Japan), and Marco Polo came this way, too.

As keepers of the crossroads, Afghans have battled wave upon wave of invaders, each time exacting bloody tribute and being bloodied themselves in turn. In the 2500 years preceding the Soviet invasion, historians have identified at least 25 dynasties who incorporated all or part of present-day Afghanistan in empires as splendid and transient as the poppy blossom. Alexander the Great founded cities here, and Genghis Khan destroyed them. In between came Parthians, Persians, Scythians, Huns, Turks, Indians and Arabs. All left their mark, and their genes, like pools in the rock after the snow had melted.

Two hundred miles from the capital, Kabul, towering Buddhas carved into red sandstone cliffs guard the Bamiyan Valley where, 18 centuries ago, thousands of monks lived in contented contemplation of the Perfect One. The Buddhas lost their faces to idol-breakers in the zealous dawn of Islam. Though it happened almost 800 years ago, a ruined citadel and the name of a village, Shahr-i-Ghulghula ('town of clamour'), recall a Mongol massacre that local Tajik villagers describe with the kind of intimate detail that makes it indistinguishable from what happened only yesterday. And so it goes, all over and all round the Hindu Kush . . .

On its western flank, where the mountains tumble into the Iranian desert, lies Herat, 'city of artists' and home to a glittering Persian culture in the 15th century. Fortified by Alexander in 330 BC, Herat was sacked by many conquerors (and the British took pot shots at its minarets in 1885).

But always it recovered, nurturing generations of painters, poets, mystics and scholars, whose tombs lent a turquoise shimmer to its pomegranate gardens. Within the city walls, the sumptuously tiled Friday Mosque and a bazaar brilliant with carpets, silver filigree and silks sustained the artistic legacy until 1979, when this was the scene of the first gory uprising against the Communist government. Retribution was massive, and dreamy Herat gained a new sobriquet – as 'Afghanistan's Hiroshima'.

These chapari *(portable reed huts) are summer quarters for the Taimani Aimaq people of the north. In winter, when the tribe moves south, they will switch to rectangular black tents. Afghanistan lies within the range of both the Arabian-style tent and the Asian yurt, and this results in many variations of nomadic habitat.*

Unruly, free and insolent . . .

Afghanistan means Land of the Afghan, but strictly speaking there is no such thing as an Afghan; it is the name used by other Afghans to describe the dominant ethnic group – and to confuse matters further, that group calls itself Pashtun, and is known to the outside world as Pathan. Besides the Pashtun, there are more than 20 other kinds of Afghan, speaking as many as 30 languages, each group, and even the tribes within each group, jealous of its differences and resentful of authority. Certain Pashtun tribes claim mythical descent from the Biblical Saul and Nebuchadnezzar, while the blue-eyed Nuristani of the remote eastern mountains like to trace their ancestry back to the army of Alexander the Great. The Hazara of the central highlands similarly claim descent from Genghis Khan's Mongols, which does nothing for their popularity. Distrust is general and mutual. Tajiks, the second-largest ethnic group, have a saying: 'Trust a snake before a harlot, and a harlot before a Pashtun.'

The word Afghan may come from a Persian word meaning 'noisy' or 'wailing', and certainly Afghanistan has been referred to at various times as Land of the Unruly, Land of the Free, even Land of the Insolent. In one of the few early references, a 14th-century Arab traveller grumbled about 'a tribe of Persians called Afghans' who 'hold mountains and defiles and are mostly robbers'. The Afghans saw it differently, and in the 17th-century warrior-poet Khushal Khan Khattak they found their cultural ideal.

When not fighting other Pashtun or the Mongols, Khushal wrote passionate poetry, lots of it, about love and bravery; the wonders of nature and the foibles of man, and how mighty the Pashtun would be if only they could unite. His wish was granted in 1747, when the last Persian conqueror was assassinated and a Pashtun warrior, Ahmad Khan, managed to unite the whole region under his leadership for the first time. For the next 230 years the Durrani tribe, which he founded, ruled Afghanistan. Even so, unity was always precarious and it took 19th-century British and Russian imperial rivalry to create the semblance of a nation out of what the British, at their peril, dismissed as 'a mere collection of tribes'.

In the 20th century, Tsarist Russia's successor, the Soviet Union, was also to taste the wrath of the Afghan tribespeople during its nine-year occupation of the land. In late December 1979 Soviet forces launched their invasion; on February 15, 1989, the Afghans got their country back. For months, columns of Soviet tanks,

The sack-like chadri *with embroidered eye mask and flowing pleats began to disappear from Kabul in 1959, but was then perpetuated by rural women who felt the custom to be sophisticated and citified.*

Carpets – an important export – are mainly woven in the north and west of Afghanistan. Even the most exquisite Turkoman rug will have one flaw constructed into the design, in respect of the fact that only Allah is perfect. Just arrived in Kabul, these rugs have been washed in the river to check for colourfastness.

trucks and troop carriers had been withdrawing across the Amu Darya (Oxus) River, their headlights full on and horns blaring. Now there was only one man left: the commander, General Boris Gromov. Under a bright winter sun, he climbed out of a jeep and, shoulders erect and without once looking back, strode to the far side of the bridge. The invasion was over, but not the war.

Afghanistan was dismembered, but the pieces kept on fighting. Of its estimated 15 million population, up to a third were in exile, and millions more had been uprooted from their homes. Green flags fluttered over hundreds of thousands of graves; villages lay in ruins, orchards and terraced hillsides had reverted to wilderness, and mountain tracks were littered with mines. The country was a checkerboard of rivalries and alliances, while from exile in Pakistan seven Islamic leaders vied for control of the rebel arms flow. Conquering Kabul took three more years, and left most questions unanswered.

Beyond the Khyber Pass

Kabul lies more than a mile high, beneath a panorama of snow-capped mountains that rise for miles more. It guards the intersection of two valleys: one points to Pakistan through the Khyber Pass, the treacherous defile that inspired a thousand tales of derring-do in the days of the British Raj.

The dust drifting in the sunlight acts as a multiple

Afghans enjoy all forms of hunting, including falconry. These rapacious pets have to be trained from the fledgling stage for their exacting role.

Their shoes off, and ensconced on a companionable carpet, friends and strangers trade gossip in a teahouse in Herat.

prism that illuminates the blue-domed Pul-i Khesti Mosque in a peculiarly sparkling light, and etches crumbling city walls set into a rocky mountain spur. Four yards thick and ten yards high, and dating from the 5th century AD, the walls – even within living memory – looked out over a broad valley floor filled with orchards and vineyards. Now the city spills across the precious level ground, surging over ridges in folds of concrete and dung-brown clay. In its midst, the curling Kabul River provides dubious domestic services, including car washes and laundry, to a population that quadrupled to an estimated 2 million during the Soviet occupation of the 1980s, when this was a comparatively secure, if jittery, haven amid the devastation of a ruthless war.

Honking yellow and black taxis nudge through crowds whose faces Alexander the Great would recognise: Uzbeks with high cheekbones and wide-apart eyes; Turkmens with the look of Chinese warlords; hawk-nosed Pashtuns, swarthy Baluchs . . . a mass of bobbing heads all the more recognisable because headgear is the last piece of clothing to resist Westernisation. The amazing variety of styles in cap (*kolah*) or turban cloth (*lungi*) not only distinguish a Tajik from an Aimaq, but also identify clans within the groups. The longer the *lungi*, the more fashionable; often a man's turban cloth will be yards longer than he is tall. The Pashtuns dangle a loose end over the shoulder; others usually tuck it in. The *lungi* has many uses: it protects a man from blows, incidental or otherwise, and from sand or snowstorms when wrapped around the face; it provides a pouch for small objects, and snacks like raisins can be tucked into the loose end; it makes a handy rope, and even finds a use in some games. A boy's first *lungi*, like his first rifle, is a symbol of manhood.

Baggy pants, loose shirt to the knees, and often a *waskat* – a fancy waistcoat – sometimes contribute to a comic brigand look, and purchases from Kabul's second-hand clothes bazaars complete the effect. For many years, Afghanistan has been a paradise of old

Tea is the national beverage, green or black according to season or individual taste, an indispensable accompaniment to social and business activity. The teahouse (left) is a male preserve except in major centres, where segregated facilities may be provided.

clothes, shipped by the ton from the United States and elsewhere, and many a US 8th Air Force or First Marine Division tunic, complete with stars and bars, has ended its days on martial Afghan shoulders. The Red Army became unwilling contributors to the trade – fur cap and Red Star being particularly popular trophies of war – but to the British must go the dubious honour of creating the market in the first place.

The Great Game

On August 7, 1839, the British Army of the Indus – 19,000 men, 40,000 camels and 38,000 camp followers – invaded Afghanistan through Kandahar in the south and went on to seize Kabul, where they installed a puppet king. Alarmed that Tsarist Russia had its eyes set on India, Britain was determined to control the high ground of the Hindu Kush.

It was, at first, a glittering occupation. The officers sent for their wives, who arrived with crystal chandeliers, fine wines, gowns and hundreds of servants. There were cricket, racing, dinners and balls, boating, ice skating in winter, and enormous regret when the Queen's 16th Lancers were posted back to India with the best polo ponies. But conquest turned to catastrophe when hostile tribes laid siege to the garrison and supplies ran low. On January 6, 1842, 16,500 troops and civilians set forth on a harrowing death march through snowbound passes and a gauntlet of fired-up tribesmen. Only one Briton, an army surgeon named William Brydon, and a few Indian Sepoys reached Jalalabad 13 days later.

Retribution of sorts was exacted by a flying column of 8000 men who forced the Khyber Pass for the first time in history, seized Kabul, and blew up the bazaar before beating a retreat. But the Russian threat remained an obsession – Rudyard Kipling called this rivalry 'The Great Game' – and British forces were back in 1879 to set up a buffer protectorate. Again they met with tribal fury, and suffered a further humiliating defeat at the Battle of Maiwand, when a legendary Pashtun heroine named Malalai used her veil as a standard and rallied the warriors by shouting this *landay* (couplet):

Young love, if you do not die at Maiwand
By Allah, you are being saved only as a token of our shame.

Malalai was not the first hot-blooded Afghan lady to leap out of purdah and on to a horse to confront the dumbfounded soldiers of Queen Victoria, for as another landay had it:

Give me two things, then let the British come:
A gun to fight with that won't jam; a girl to fight next to, who will love.

Standing room only! The moutar *(truck) frequently does double duty as a bus in Afghanistan. Though pack animals are being steadily supplanted by motor transport, they proved their worth after the Soviet invasion, when the roads were too dangerous to use and the resistance fighters had to be supplied.*

Ruz-e bazaar *(market day) is an important focus of life in a land where villages have no shops. Here at Tashqurghan, in the far north, there is a daily market. Activity peaks towards the end of summer, when crops are harvested.*

It would be another 40 years before it dawned on Whitehall that the Afghans could be relied upon to protect themselves from outsiders, if not from one another. A hundred years late, the Russians did finally arrive in 1979, having learned nothing from the lessons of history, or the old Hindu prayer: 'From the venom of the cobra, the teeth of the tiger, and the vengeance of the Afghan – deliver us!'

The Afghan guerrillas who battled the forces of the Soviet Union to a standstill were known as *mujahidin* or warriors of the *jihad;* a holy war called against unbelievers – foes of Islam. A good Muslim is bound, as an article of his faith, to take part in a *jihad,* so long as it is properly constituted, but this inevitably becomes a matter of debate – as witness an attempt by Turkey's last Caliph to declare the First World War a *jihad* in alliance with the German Kaiser.

Afghanistan's religious leaders had proclaimed this *jihad* a full 20 months before the first Soviet troops came over the border, and Moscow's fateful intervention was actually in furtherance of a coup to impose a regime more sensitive to Muslim sensibilities than the first wave of local Communist revolutionaries had been. But that became a mere point of irony. Here in their midst was an alien force of atheists, and that rendered the *jihad* authentically holy: even the British *farangi*

(Franks) had at least been People of the Book (the Bible).

The beginnings of Afghanistan's agony could be traced back a further 50 years to the impetuosity of a king who, dazzled by the achievements of Atatürk in Turkey, strove to turn his tribal kingdom into a Western-style democracy, even to the extent of female emancipation, co-education and no more polygamy. King Amanullah (he preferred that title to the old-style 'Amir') rigged out tribal elders in black tie and tails, but went too far when he had his own Queen Suraiya unveil in public. Such was the furore that a Tajik bandit nicknamed Bacha Saqao ('son of a water-carrier') was able to seize the capital and hold it for nine months before a Pashtun *lashkar* (tribal army) could unseat him. Amanullah was retired to Italy, and women restored to their colourful *chadri* sacks.

Thirty years on, in 1959, the barefaced experiment was risked again, and the seclusion of women – purdah – was formally abolished. Traditionalists were as outraged as ever, but this time the move came as part of a step-by-step 'New Democracy' programme that by 1965 had transformed Afghanistan, in theory at least, into a parliamentary democracy. In Kabul outside foreign-aid programmes stimulated a heady tempo of new ideas that were promulgated and heatedly debated by a burgeoning but still tiny educated class with increasingly divergent viewpoints. Outside the capital, however, unrest and opposition to the government grew, spurred by a backlash against women's rights, on the one hand, and a two-year drought, on the other. The drought and the subsequent famine cost the lives of between 50,000 and half a million Afghans, depending on who was to be believed. A coup in 1973 ended the monarchy and was followed by another on April 27, 1978, ending 230 years of rule by the Durrani, and installing in its place the Khalq (People) Party, a Marxist splinter group whose frenzy alarmed even Moscow. Opponents were jailed, tortured, and hundreds

Along the lower valleys and around oasis towns such as Herat, Afghanistan's orchards produce fruit of rare quality and variety. As well as being sold locally, it is exported to neighbouring countries, especially the former Soviet Union.

Opposite page:
Like a detail from some 19th-century Orientalist painting, this butcher's booth is typically meagre in its range of meat. Though Afghanistan is a stock-rearing country and dairy products play a major role in their diet, Afghans are not great meat-eaters.

Fare is as simple as facilities in rural restaurants such as this one at Tashkqurghan, where the speciality is fried fish.

executed. Mullahs – Koranic teachers – were persecuted and denounced as 'brothers of Satan', and Kabul was painted red – literally, until the paint supply ran out. The tiny middle class of professionals began to flee to Pakistan, the vanguard of a mass exodus.

The Khalq's biggest mistake was to declare sweeping reforms, such as land redistribution, with no sensitivity or forethought. It decreed an upper limit on the *shir-baha* (bride price) paid by a groom's family, and set a minimum marriage age of 16 for girls and 18 for boys; henceforth nobody was to be obliged to marry against their will. The idea was to curb peasant indebtedness and to enhance the dignity of women, but it struck at the bedrock of traditional culture. To break the mullahs' grip on the peasantry, a mass literacy campaign was launched in the villages, with party propaganda as the teaching material. The first fatal clash is said to have occurred after party zealots attempted to drag some women out of their homes to attend a literacy class – a violation of everything traditional culture stood for.

Within a year there was open rebellion, starting in Herat, where the Islamic revolution of the Ayatollah Khomeini in neighbouring Iran had helped to foment a very different kind of radicalism. Mobs burned and butchered, and army units mutinied and joined them. By the spring of 1979, only the main road from Herat to Kabul was safe, and by June there was trouble in the capital itself. In true Afghan fashion, it was every tribe for itself, with the Hazara of the central highlands and the Nuristani in the east as intent on regaining lost autonomy as in opposing godless government. The Tajiks were quick to follow, and the brutality of the regime in putting down the revolt only swelled rebel ranks. The reformers at first avoided tangling with the powerful Pashtuns, but once the harvest was in, Pashtun khans also took up arms – sometimes settling old scores against one another.

The fateful Soviet invasion in late December was intended in part to eliminate the ruthless Khalq leadership and install more amenable Marxists, but the sight of Red Army tanks rolling south shocked as nothing else could. Mosques were used to call the faithful to arms, and at night entire populations took to the rooftops, crying 'Allah-o-Akbar' – God is great – and chanting in unison the Muslim call to prayer. The purged and apologetic regime hauled down its red flag and restored the Afghan tricolour of red, black and Islamic green, brought some non-Marxists into the government, and wooed the mullahs with money and a flurry of mosque construction, but the rage was much too great to be contained.

mostly country people hoping to escape famine and the pounding of their villages and crops as the guerrilla war raged around them.

Clearly, such an influx put a huge strain on the city, which had never, in any case, been a place of outstanding architectural beauty, and which would also experience a fair share of the fighting and

Opposite page:
The shrine of Ali draws thousands of pilgrims to Mazir-e Sharif for Nawruz, the Afghan New Year. All evidence points to Ali being buried in Iraq, but Afghans stick to their own beliefs.

Saintly to some, a rogue to others, the malang *is feared and respected by unsophisticated Afghans, who look to him to intercede with Allah, or to provide the right charm or amulet to ward off accident and disease. Gradual modernisation of the country and a surge of Islamic radicalism provoked by the Soviet invasion have jeopardised these holy wanderers.*

Babur's city

The explosion of that anger has affected all of Afghanistan – not to mention spilling over among neighbours such as Pakistan. And not surprisingly Kabul, the capital, has borne the brunt of many of the country's swings in fortune. In 1978, for example, it was a comparatively modest city of some 600,000 inhabitants; ten years later its population had more than tripled to around 2 million. The new arrivals were

bombardments, both before and after the eventual Soviet withdrawal. Shanty towns consisting of hastily improvised dwellings put together with a few bricks and roofs often made from the branches of trees swarmed up the rocky mountainsides around the city, mingling with the tents and flocks of nomadic herdsmen. In a desperate attempt to look after the refugees, the government absorbed as many as possible into a bloated bureaucracy – leaving a crisis of state expenditure that future governments would have to try to untangle.

And yet, for all such difficulties, Kabul is by no

Roaming the roof of the world with their woolly-coated, sure-footed yaks – who cannot stand the summer heat of the lower valleys – Kyrgyz nomads batten down for the night in an ooee, *a rounded, galeproof version of the* yurt *and tend their babies in traditional bamboo cribs (right). In 1980, most Kyrgyz were driven from the remote Pamir passes by the war, and took refuge in Pakistan.*

means without charm. In the first place, it could hardly boast a more spectacular setting, spread out over an open basin in the mountains, 6900 feet above sea level, with the peaks of the Kuh-e Asmai and Kuh-e Sherdawaza ranges rising majestically on either side. It is a place of extremes, impossibly hot and dusty in summer, with all sound muted in winter by a thick mantle of snow. But these extremes, too, have their charm. One man who appreciated them was the 16th-century founder of the Moghul Empire in India, Zahir ud din Muhammad, better known as Babur, descendant of both Tamerlane and Genghis Khan, whose first conquest in his rise from dispossessed prince to mighty emperor was Kabul in 1504. 'From Kabul it is but a day's journey to places where snow never falls,' he wrote in his memoirs, 'while in two hours you can reach places where the snow never melts . . . In the region around Kabul, you can find the fruits of two climates, growing abundantly and close at hand. Among the fruit of the cooler regions . . . are grapes, pomegranates, apricots, apples, quinces, peaches, plums, jujube fruits, almonds and all kinds of nuts . . . As for the fruit of the hot regions, you find the orange, bitter orange, amluk and sugar cane . . . The rhubarb, quinces, plums and cucumbers of Kabul are excellent.' Such was Babur's affection for Kabul that he asked to be buried there – his tomb survives in the city's western outskirts, near the ruined walls of the ancient Bala Hissar fortress, among gardens where once the great monarch liked to stroll, and where he himself planted trees and flowers.

In Kabul's bazaar, meanwhile, evidence abounds of the district's continuing fertility and the skills of its craftsmen. Since the original covered bazaar was destroyed during the British raid of 1842, the bazaar has spread over a teaming warren of narrow, unpaved streets and alleys, where in summer stallholders try vainly to control the clouds of dust by sprinkling them with water. The war has certainly taken its toll on Kabul as a whole, but here you might almost forget it. Carpet-sellers offer richly woven rugs from the regions around Mazar-e Sharif and Herat; jewellers (*koladoz*) sit out on the pavement beside glass cases displaying silver necklaces and pendants studded with local semi-precious stones; dyers grind their coloured powders and

The Afghan does not live on nan *(bread) alone, but sometimes comes close to it – in fact, the term* nan *has come to refer to food in general. This Kyrgyz woman is baking with a portable iron griddle of a kind commonly used by nomads. The fire is lit underneath. Afghan food is a pleasing mixture of Turkish, Iranian, Indian, Tibetan and Chinese influences – as mixed as the rest of its culture.*

stir the steaming pots in which fabrics will be dipped to emerge in the brilliant hues beloved of the Afghans. There are also some more unusual trades: the *patragars*, for example, who mend broken china (an important skill over the last troubled decade) and the *kona froushi*, the second-hand clothes' sellers. Turbaned barbers sit cross-legged at the streetside with their bare-headed clients squatting, heads bowed, in front of them. In summer, water-bearers (*saqaos*) stagger down the alleys, carrying brimming water skins. In winter, after a fall of snow, the streets echo to the cry of the snow-clearers (*barf pak*). At most times of the year, there is the cacophony of honking trucks, shouting rickshaw drivers, tinkling bicycle bells, the bleating of sheep and goats, the braying of donkeys and the more restrained grunts of camels.

Afghan weddings involve elaborate rituals through two stages of betrothal and three days of celebration and ceremony, paid for by the family of the groom. Among Turkoman tribes of the north, the procession that leads the bride to the home of her husband . . .

. . . is preceded by a camel loaded with fine carpets that add to the high cost of a wedding. Marriage can drive a man into lifelong debt, given the high cost of borrowing.

Sacred doves, witches and an abominable snowman

Under the rules of a *jihad*, slain warriors proceed directly to Paradise, and during the Soviet occupation this was a great consolation to many grieving Afghan widows, mothers and sisters. As the fighting progressed, wonderful stories circulated of *mujahidin* corpses which did not decompose, and of flights of birds stopping bombing raids.

Though most Afghans are devout Sunni Muslims and pray towards Mecca five times each day, here – as elsewhere in the Muslim world – their faith has absorbed a variety of local beliefs and practices. Supernatural creatures abound, and so do good and bad spirits, and the illiterate farmer-mullah of a remote village may be more practised in spells and charms (*jadu* and *taawiz*) to combat black magic (*seher*) and witches (*koftarha*) than in the formal rites of his religion. *Jinn* are spirits that possess the living, causing mischief and sometimes insanity, so they have to be exorcised. Then there are *arwa*, ghosts of the distraught dead, beautiful fairies called *pari*, and horned giants. Nuristan has its own abominable snowman. Wandering the land are persons called *malang*, holy men believed to have been touched by the hand of God, and as such half honoured, half feared; a mother who approaches a *malang* for help will not permit her children to go near him, even if they are the subject of the consultation. Occasionally a *malang* goes naked, or wears women's clothes; usually they wear coats made to their own eccentric design, of many colours and cloths, and jangling with tin jewellery and *taawiz* (charms); they carry a stick to fend off dogs, and a wooden bowl. Most are Sufis, learned to some degree in techniques of mystic ecstasy, and given to talking in tongues.

With the opening up of the country, and the rise of a radical Islam striving for purity in the aftermath of the great *jihad*, the *malangs'* days seem numbered, but old ways die hard – and what the mullah cannot fix, the *malang* just might. In practice, the immemorial and the modern have a tendency to congeal, sometimes towards a commercial end. Among the most highly revered of Sufi leaders, for example, are the *pirs*, generally men of great learning as well as holiness. One *mujahidin* leader, holy enough for his bath water to be distributed to the sick, managed to combine the careers of hereditary *pir* and Kabul agent for Peugeot cars.

Sometimes a *malang* is credited with a miracle, and settles at the scene of his accomplishment. When he dies, his tomb becomes a shrine (*ziarat*) and the village acquires its personal saint as a kind of guardian angel. In theory Sunni Islam has no place for saints, which the puritanical Saudi Arabians, for example, regard as idolatry, but human needs are such that saints and shrines abound in the Muslim world. Nowhere is this more true than in Afghanistan, where a wide selection of shrines are patronised by pilgrims seeking every manner of favour, from protection against the evil eye, or bullets in a feud, to cures for mad-dog bites (near Charikar) and insanity (Jalalabad). One valley north of Kabul has 40 shrines all dedicated to fertility, including one in which women desirous of a child fondle the bones of *shahid* (*jihad* martyrs) and eat pinches of earth.

Supplicants usually leave a simple offering, sometimes a candle or piece of cloth, and a donation towards the upkeep of the shrine. Shrinekeepers also sell charms for every need. Often a *taawiz* is no more than a verse from the Koran, sealed in a little container for sewing into one's clothing, but there are also rare charms of special power, such as the bullet that wounded but did not kill.

The prime shrine is as particular to Afghanistan as is the rest of Afghan belief. Mazar-e Sharif means 'tomb of the saint', and here, on the northern plain of Turkestan, which Afghanistan shares with the former Soviet republic of Turkmenistan, Afghans flock to venerate the remains of Ali, son-in-law of the prophet, under a crimson drape within a splendid turquoise mausoleum – despite compelling evidence that Ali lies, equally venerated, 1500 miles away in Iraq.

Ali was the cause of the great schism in Islam, which led to the forming of the Shia (Party of Ali) sect. In fact, less than 20 per cent of Afghans are Shia Muslims, but such niceties are of no importance to the thousands of pilgrims (most of them Sunnis) who believe that, after his assassination, Ali's followers tied his body to the back of a white female camel, which then transported it to this very spot. How the bones were identified is unclear, but doubters are shown a Koran, said to have

The Turkoman bride in traditional gown and silver finery – a practical form of investment in a society where the banking system is limited to the major towns. The fish-shaped pendants are ancient symbols of fertility and the silver circlets are good luck charms. Many women sold their jewellery to help the mujahidin *war effort.*

been hand-written by Ali himself, and a marble stele said to have accompanied the body. Throughout the Afghan north, there are rocky outcrops and odd geological structures linked to Ali and his prowess as a dragon-slayer and mover of mountains.

Flocks of sacred white doves, plump from over-feeding, flutter and flop about the shrine – and woe betide anyone who should harm one, however accidentally, for every seventh bird is an *arwa,* who will haunt the transgressor to the end of his days. On the Afghan New Year (March 21), the *jandah* (standard) of Ali is raised in the packed courtyard of the shrine, and pilgrims scramble to touch its staff; many are crippled or diseased, hoping for a miraculous cure. After about 40 days, the standard is lowered in conjunction with the blooming of a species of red tulip, and this is marked by cheerful family gatherings, seemingly the remnant of a forgotten fertility rite that predates Islam, just as the shrine itself clearly does.

The Mazar-e Sharif festivities fill the town with merchants and tinkers of every sort, including bands of *djat* – itinerant blacksmiths, fortune-tellers, dancers and musicians of Indian origin. Once it is over, the crowds disperse aboard packed trucks and buses with a suddenness that leaves the wide streets looking forlorn.

Buzkashi *('goat-grabbing') is the national sport of Afghanistan – a combination of polo and rugby with an animal carcase as the 'ball'.*

Nomadic heritage

The pastoral nomads do not have time to pay their respects to Ali, being much too busy preparing for the spring migration. Afghanistan's nomads cherish their heritage, and the mountains still pulse to the harsh rhythms of the seasons; but a century of upheaval, border closures, and dislocation caused by war, puts the number of nomads in doubt: in the late 1970s, the estimate was about 2 million.

Moves are agreed at a meeting of the clan chiefs. The start is made by night, ideally under a full moon. The bands string out, with herds of fat-tailed sheep and goats moving along higher up the slope and the main body plodding along the valley floor. Camels, donkeys and cattle are loaded with the paraphernalia of life, from tents to tambourines; small children, chickens and puppies are also stowed aboard the swaying beasts; only the horses are spared pack duty, being strictly for riding. Large dogs with clipped tails and ears patrol the flanks.

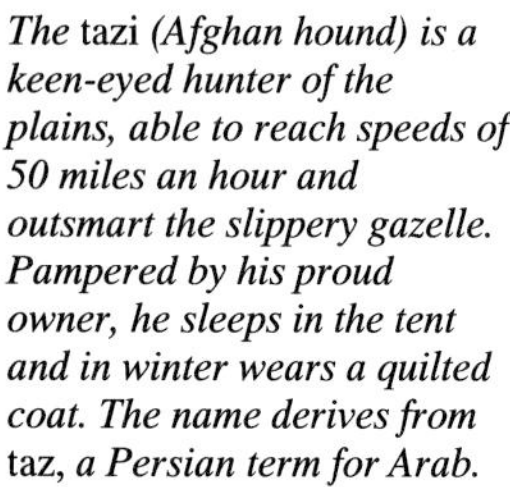

The tazi *(Afghan hound) is a keen-eyed hunter of the plains, able to reach speeds of 50 miles an hour and outsmart the slippery gazelle. Pampered by his proud owner, he sleeps in the tent and in winter wears a quilted coat. The name derives from* taz, *a Persian term for Arab.*

Scouts along the trail act as traffic controllers, keeping each group in touch with those ahead and behind, and occasionally a group will halt and graze for several days while the line adjusts itself. Subsections within each band mark their livestock with distinctive designs, often bird shaped; and some Pashtun nomads tattoo their women the same way! A band may move only two or three miles in a day, or as many as 15 when traversing a pass and barren stretch. At each night's halt, it is the women who swing into action, unloading the animals, erecting the tents, cooking; while the men mount guard, or else hire local villagers to do it for them. 'The men play at being men', the anthropologist Louis Dupree wrote. 'They sing songs of love and war. They plot blood-feud revenges and raids from their winter quarters . . .'

The relationship between the nomads and the settled villages on their lines of march has always been strained, but symbiotic: the nomads have traditionally brought news and trade goods of every description; their herds have fertilised the fields and marginal grasslands; they even acted as bankers, lending money at extortionate rates, and sometimes – the Pashtun nomads are famous for this – driving their hosts into debt and dependence. Motor transport and the extension of the road network, as well as the growth of permanent agriculture through the development of irrigation systems, must soon change things for ever, though climate and terrain would seem to dictate that some semi-nomadic lifestyles will go on.

The last idolaters

The most obdurate of all the Afghan peoples – the last to convert to Islam, yet the first to rise against Communist government – is also the most mysterious. High in a mountain pocket 150 miles north of Kabul, amid rare oak woods populated by macaque monkeys, live a people who clung fiercely to their pagan gods until finally conquered by the army of Amir Abdur Rahman in 1895. Known as the Kafirs – 'infidels' – they sent 300 cavalry to fight with Alexander the Great in 326 BC, but this is about all that is known of their history. Since many have blue eyes and blond or red hair, they are the subject of wildly romantic speculation – that they might be the ancestral stock of the Anglo-Saxons, for instance. Their languages – they have at least five, with different terms for 'mother' and 'father' in valleys less than a day's walk apart – reveal only the degree of their determined isolation.

Kafiristan was renamed Nuristan ('land of light') after its conversion, but the Nuristani have kept their

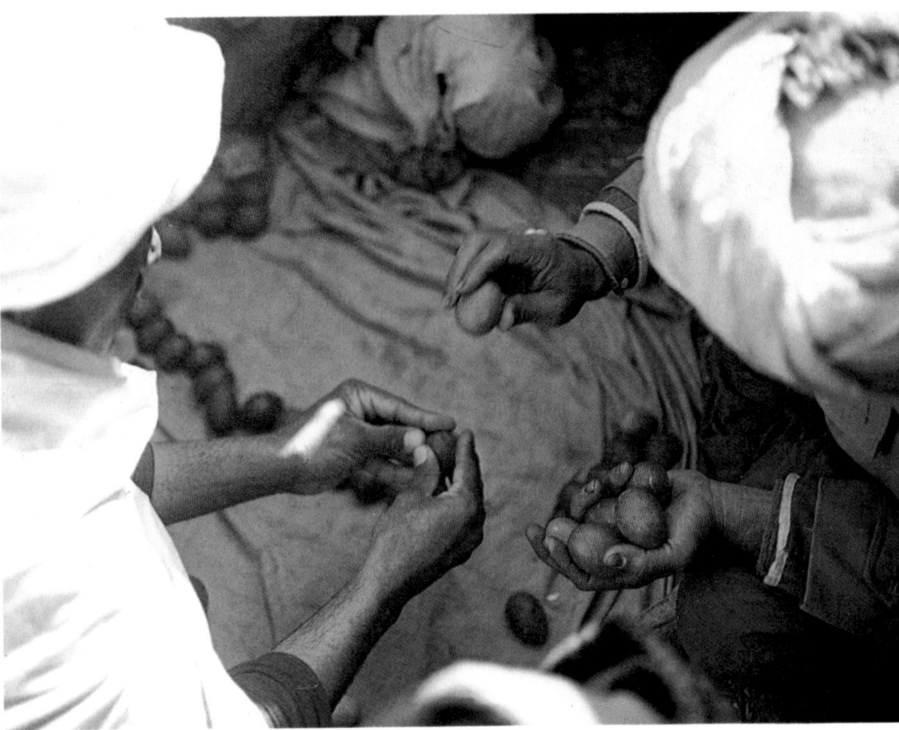

distance and their differences, from their floppy pork-pie caps (*pawkul*) – though these have been widely adopted elsewhere in Afghanistan since 1980 and came to be a kind of emblem of the *mujahidin* resistance – to their feudal social arrangements. Villages cling to steep mountainsides, the wooden houses effectively serried ramparts, each flat roof a terrace for the house above it, bedecked in season with apricots and beans, mulberries and walnuts spread out to dry. These homes have tables and chairs, another distinction, since the rest of Afghanistan sits on the floor. House and contents are built by an artisan class known as the *bari,* formerly slaves, who also provide the cobblers who make the Nuristanis' fine hide boots, the smiths, weavers, potters, carpenters, carvers . . .

The women tend patches of millet and barley in the

Afghans will bet on anything – even on which egg will break when two are bumped together. Tokhm-jangi *(eggfighting) is popular with youngsters during the New Year festivities. To prepare them for battle, the eggs are first boiled, then painted in bright colours.*

Dogfighting is officially discouraged, but it is popular with gamblers. To lessen vulnerability, the dogs' ears and tails are lopped off. The combat is bloody, though owners step in when a dog seems in serious danger.

valley below, hauling home the harvest in tall baskets strapped to their backs. Freed of all duties – their prized goat herds being tended by others – the aristocratic Nuristani men in dashing knee-length pantaloons and leggings can relax drinking tea, but apparent indolence is deceptive in a warrior culture. When Communist militants abducted some of their tribal elders, the Nuristani rose as one, and within a year of the 1978 coup had 'liberated' virtually all of their homeland.

Buzkashi – the sport of Afghans

Picture a dozen plunging, wild-eyed stallions colliding around a bloodied animal carcase, their sweating riders flaying away with short whips as scores of other turbaned figures wheel round and round the confusion of dust and flying hoofs.

'*Wardar! Namani!*' Pick it up! Don't let it go!'

Hanging from one stirrup, a *chapandaz* (master rider) manages to grab and hoist the gruesome burden, jamming it between his leg and the pommel of his saddle; then he rears his horse and tries to kick free of the melee.

A game of *buzkashi* – 'goat-grab' – has just begun. A rugged relative of polo invented on the steppes of Central Asia, this is the national sport of Afghanistan, and as appropriate in spirit as baseball is to America, or cricket to England. The rules are few, though lately there have been attempts to reduce casualties by posting mounted umpires, limiting the size of teams, and penalising contestants who too blatantly use their whip on an opponent, or otherwise try to force him off his horse. In northern Afghanistan, enthusiasts still prefer their *buzkashi* the old-fashioned way, and games involving more than 1000 horsemen have been known.

It used to be that a prisoner-of-war might be placed in the starting circle, but nowadays it is usual to use the headless carcase of a goat or calf. At a rifle shot, or blast on a whistle, each side's *chapandaz* whirl in formation around the carcase until one of them seizes and secures it, and the chase is on. To score a goal, the carcase has to be carried around a turning point some distance away, then returned and dropped into the original circle. Sometimes two or three riders have a grip on the carcase at one time; whips clenched in teeth, they heave and wrestle while clinging to their mounts by their stirrups. If the carcase falls apart, the rider holding the largest piece is judged to be the one in control of 'the ball'. That need to hold on and not let go seems a fitting symbol for the Afghan people as a whole, in their sheer, dogged tenacity against all that the centuries have thrown against them.

The camel is not exclusive to the sand desert, and can carry loads of up to 300 pounds over the icy passes of the northern Hindu Kush. This bad-tempered, invaluable beast is the subject of an immense body of folklore in the Middle East. For example: Allah (God) has 100 names, or attributes, and man knows only 99. The camel knows the 100th, but will not reveal it – which helps to explain its haughty demeanour.

Gazetteer

Turkey

The history of Turkey as a nation dates back to the 15th century, when the Ottoman Turks conquererd Constantinople (present-day Istanbul) and created the great Ottoman Empire on the ruins of Byzantium. After the First World War a reborn Turkey emerged out of the collapse of the Ottoman Empire. Its leader, Kemal Atatürk, dragged Turkish Society out of its centuries-old rut and made Turkey a modern state. He overthrew many cherished Turkish traditions, and ended Islam's status as the official religion.

Colonisation of Anatolia: c. 6000 BC

The Anatolian plateau, which forms the heart of Turkey, was settled c. 6000 BC by peoples from the east, who established primitive farming communities.

Hittite invaders swept into the Anatolian peninsula c. 2000 BC. Their empire lasted for nearly eight centuries. Revolts, combined with attacks by Greek migrants, led to its collapse c. 1220 BC.

Greek settlement: c. 600 BC

After the fall of the Hittites, two new kingdoms, Phrygia and Lydia, were founded by Indo-Europeans. Civilisation reached an advanced stage in Lydia. In the 7th century BC the Lydians minted the first known coinage.

At about this time, Greek settlements were founded along the Anatolian coast, but by 550 BC many of these had fallen under Lydian control. Lydia itself was conquered by the Persians c. 546 BC, and the Greek settlements came under Persian rule. Persian dominance lasted until Persia itself was overthrown by Alexander the Great 200 years later. After his death, Macedonian immigrants established control in much of Anatolia and Greek civilisation gradually spread over the entire area. The Romans began to make inroads into Anatolia in 133 BC, but it was not until 67 BC that the region was brought fully under their rule.

Byzantine Empire

When the Roman Empire was divided by Diocletian in the 3rd century AD, Byzantium, a Greek city, became the capital of the eastern empire. In AD 330, the Christian emperor, Constantine, moved his capital there from Rome, rebuilding the city and renaming it Constantinople. The Byzantine Empire, as the eastern empire became known, outlasted the Roman Empire in the west, surviving until 1453. Its 'golden age' was in the 6th century AD when it spread westwards to Spain, northwards to the Danube and along the coast of North Africa.

From the 10th century onwards, the empire gradually contracted under attack from Turkic-speaking tribes – first the Seljuks and then the Ottomans. By the early 14th century, the once-mighty Byzantine Empire had shrunk to Constantinople and the area immediately surrounding it. The city was finally captured by the Ottomans in 1453 under the leadership of Mehmet II. The last emperor, Constantine XI, was killed in battle.

Expansion and decline

Ottoman expansion continued after the fall of Constantinople. Its highest point came under Suleiman I, known as 'The Magnificent' (1520-66). The Turks controlled Asia Minor, the Arabian peninsula, Egypt, North Africa and the Balkans; their armies threatened Vienna. The tide began to turn when Spanish and Venetian fleets won the Battle of Lepanto (1571). During the 17th and 18th centuries, Turkey was attacked by both Austria and Russia. The country fell into decay under a long line of incompetent sultans.

The army, too, was giving trouble, especially the élite fighting corps, the Janissaries. Originally its members had been Christian captives who were converted to Islam and then bound by an oath of loyalty to the sultan. But in time, the Janissaries became corrupt; they controlled the sultan rather than served him.

War of Greek independence

In 1821, Greece – part of the Ottoman Empire since 1460 – rose against the Turks, who suppressed the revolt with great cruelty. In 1826 Britain and Russia agreed to co-operate in securing Greek independence, which Turkey acknowledged by the Treaty of Adrianople (1829). In the 1830s Egypt, too, threw off Turkish control. By 1840, Turkey had become known as 'the sick man of Europe'. The country's rulers had already realised the need for reforms, but these were opposed by orthodox Muslims, who believed that the laws of Islam could never be altered, as well as by extreme nationalists, who disapproved of all foreign influences.

TURKEY AT A GLANCE

Area 300,946 square miles

Population 52,340,000

Capital Ankara

Government Parliamentary republic

Currency Lira = 100 kurus (piastres)

Languages Turkish (official), Arabic, Greek, Circassian, Armenian, Yiddish, Kurdish

Religion Muslim (98%)

Climate Mediterranean on the coast, continental inland; average temperature in Ankara ranges from -4 to 4°C (25-39°F) in January to 15-31°C (59-88°F) in August

Main primary products Wheat, barley, maize, cotton, sugar beet, pulses, cattle, sheep, goats, tobacco, fruit (olives, nuts, figs), vegetables, fish; coal, lignite, iron, crude oil, chrome, boron, copper

Major industries Agriculture, steel, textiles, tobacco and food processing, oil refining, chemicals, paper, fishing, mining

Main exports Textiles, cotton, nuts, fruit, tobacco, cereals, pulses

Annual income per head (US$) 1350

Population growth (per thous/yr) 21

Life expectancy (yrs) Male 60 **Female** 64

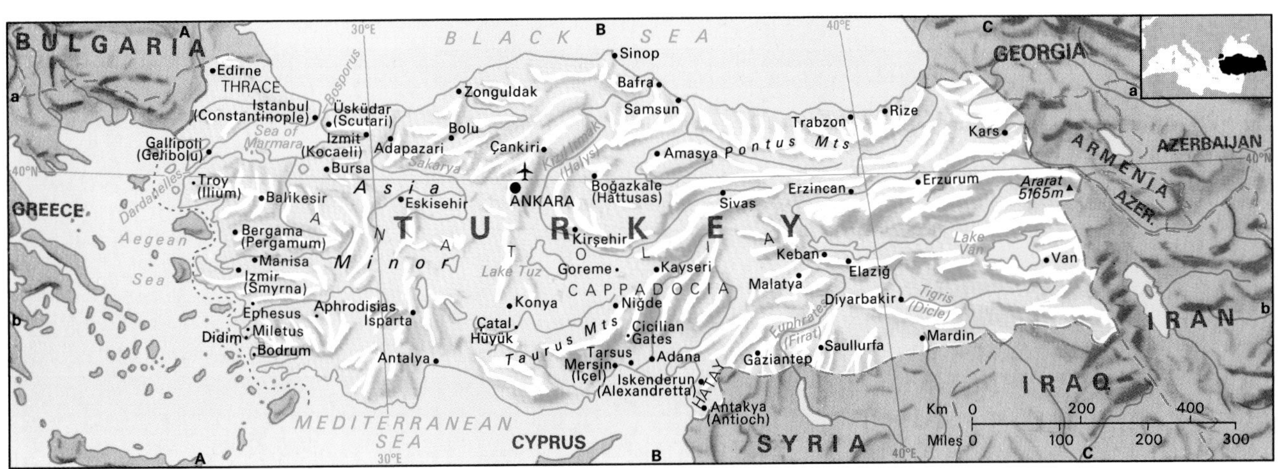

Crimean War: 1854-6

As part of its aggressive policy towards Turkey, Russia claimed the right to 'protect' Christian subjects of the sultan. In 1853 Russian troops occupied Turkish territory on the Black Sea, and the sultan declared war. Public opinion in Britain regareded the idea of the Russians capturing Constantinople as disastrous. France, too, wanted to keep the Russian navy out of the Mediterranean. Britain and France went to the sultan's aid (1854) and, after an inconclusive campaign in the Crimea, peace was agreed in 1856.

'Peace with honour': 1878

Europe was horrified when in 1875 and 1876 the Turks brutally crushed revolts in Herzegovina, Bosnia and Bulgaria. Russia stepped in, and an independent Bulgaria stretching from the Black Sea to the Aegean was created. Britain supported Turkey. A congress at Berlin in 1878 settled the issue: the Turks lost some territory – a smaller Bulgaria was formed – but their remaining empire was guaranteed. The British prime minister, Disraeli, claimed that this settlement had brought 'peace with honour', but Turkey had, in effect, lost more prestige.

Reform and revolution

Reformers, led by Midhat Pasha, forced Sultan Abdul Hamid II to introduce a democratic constitution in 1876. But Abdul Hamid soon re-established despotic power.

In the 1890's, the Committee of Union and Progress was set up by youthful reformers who became known as the 'Young Turks'; among them was Mustafa Kemal, who later became the nation's president. In 1908, troops revolted and the sultan had to restore the constitution of 1876. His attempt to organise a counter-revolution failed; he abdicated and the Young Turks took over.

The regime was soon threatened by the Balkan powers, who defeated Turkey in wars in 1912 and 1913. As a result, it looked to Germany for support. German officers were sent to train the army, and in 1914 Turkey signed a secret alliance with Germany against Russia.

First World War: 1914-18

Turkey allied itself with Germany in the First World War. Allied forces landed at Gallipoli in 1915 – a costly attempt at invasion that ended in failure.

Elsewhere, however, Turkey met little but defeat, losing the last remnants of its vast empire. British armies commanded by General Allenby – aided by Arab guerrillas under T.E. Lawrence ('Lawrence of Arabia') – drove the Turks out of Palestine and Syria.

In 1920, the last sultan, Mehmet VI, accepted the Treaty of Sèvres, which reduced Turkey to the level of a minor power. Much territory was given to Greece. This provoked a nationalist uprising; the sultan was deposed and the Greeks were driven out. Allied occupation forces were eventually withdrawn.

Atatürk's rule

The leader of the nationalist revolt, Mustafa Kemal, a soldier who had distinguished himself at Gallipoli, became the first president of the republic in 1923 and ruled virtually as a dictator until 1938. He was the father of modern Turkey, bringing a backward Muslim state into the modern world. To Westernise his country, he separated religion and the state, abolished polygamy, banned men from wearing the fez (the brimless felt cap of Muslims) and discouraged women from using the veil. He sent everyone under 40 to classes to learn a new Latin alphabet for the Turkish language. He decreed that everyone should have a surname. Kemal chose the name Atatürk (father of the Turks). The capital was moved from Constantinople (now Istanbul) to Ankara in 1923.

After Atatürk's death in 1938, his appointed successors held power until 1950. Turkey was neutral in the Second World War until 1945, when it declared war on Germany. Turks fought alongside Americans in the Korean War, and the USA still maintains military bases in Turkey. After the war Russia pressed claims to Turkish territory. America and Britain supported Turkey with arms and financial aid and it joined NATO in 1951.

Turkey today

The Democratic party won the country's first free elections in 1950 and ruled until overthrown by the military in 1960. Coalition governments, unrest and political instability followed. During the 1970's neither of the leading political parties was able to hold a clear majority in parliament. Conservative Suleyman Demirel, head of the Justice Party, and Bulent Ecevit, leader of the Republican People's Party (RPU), alternated in serving as prime minister.

The Greek-led overthrow of the Cyprus government in July 1974 caused Turkey to invade the island with 40,000 troops. With inflation reaching 100 per cent, the economy bankrupted by the costs of the Cyprus invasion and a decade of terrorism threatening to break into civil war, the military seized the country in 1980. All political activity was banned until 1983. The conservative Motherland Party won a majority in the 1983 election and its leader, Turgut Ozal, became prime minister. By the end of 1985, martial law had been removed from 17 of the country's 67 provinces, but thousands of Turks remained in prison, and many groups, including unions and student and professional associations, were barred from political activities.

The population has become a rich blend of peoples and cultures. They are of Mediterranean stock in the west, and Armenians from the Caspian area in the east; while in the south-east there are several million kurds, ethnically close to the Iranians. Ninety per cent of the people speak Turkish, a language of many dialects which was changed from Arabic script to Roman alphabet in 1928. Most are Muslims.

The country has a substantial industrial sector, good agricultural land and mineral resources, including large deposits of chrome. Industry is mainly around Istanbul and Ankara, and in the south-east near Adana and Iskenderun. Manufactures include iron, steel, textiles, motor vehicles, petrochemicals, processed food and Turkey's famous carpets, tobacco, meerschaum pipes and pottery. The two great rivers of the Middle East, the Tigris and Euphrates, both rise in Turkey, and hydroelectric plants supply half of the country's energy needs.

Encouraged by the government, farmers have achieved the best rate of agricultural production in the Middle East outside Israel. Despite its dryness, the Anatolian plateau is the granary of Turkey. The main crops are cerals, rice, cotton, fruit and tobacco, and most of the country's sheep, goats and cattle are raised there.

Mechanisation and an increasing population have forced many peasants to seek jobs in the overcrowded cities. Others have emigrated. About 1.5 million Turks, for instance, work in West Germany, while some 175,000 are in the oil-rich Middle Eastern states. Their remittances home help the country's continual struggle to pay for its imports.

Israel

With the proclamation of the State of Israel in 1948, an ancient Jewish dream became a reality. For almost 2000 years after they were displaced by the Romans from their homeland, the dream of a return to the 'Promised Land' of Palestine never ceased to burn in the minds of the Jewish people. The dream was sustained by their religion, which spoke of a Messiah who would lead them back from exile, and intensified by cruel persecution.

Not all Jews suffered during the long centuries of the Diaspora (dispersion). Some groups merged successfully into the life of their adoptive countries, becoming leaders of commerce and industry, and making contributions to thought, science and the arts which were out of all proportion to their numbers. But for most Jews of the Diaspora, living precariously in ghettos, persecution was a more usual fate.

Since independence, Israel has been in constant conflict with its encircling Arab neighbours, who deny that the Israelis have any right to the soil of Palestine; four times the dispute has erupted into war. By the end of the six-day war of 1967 the Israelis had gained territory which stretched across the Sinai Peninsula to the banks of the Suez Canal, and included the West Bank of the River Jordan and Syria's Golan Heights. War broke out again in 1973, when Egypt and Syria attacked the Israelis in a bid to win back their lost territory.

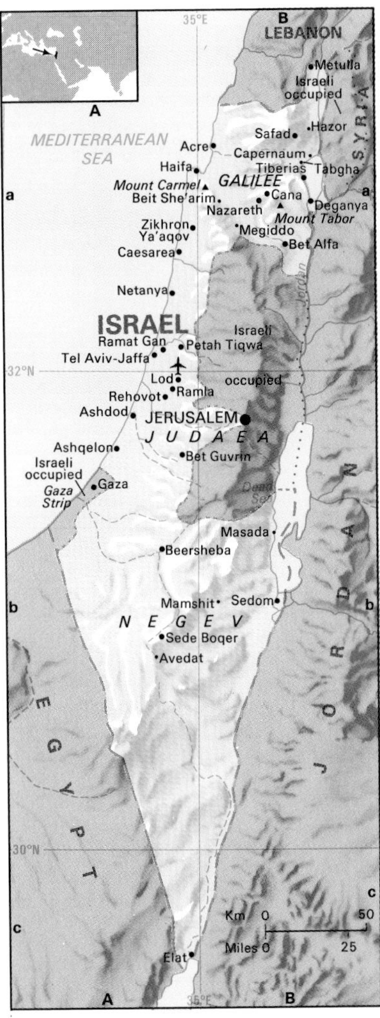

ISRAEL AT A GLANCE

Area 7992 square miles as defined in the 1949 armistice agreements
Population 4,822,000
Capital Jerusalem
Government Parliamentary republic
Currency Shekel
Languages Hebrew, Arabic
Religions Jewish (83%), Muslim (11%), C hristian/others 6%
Climate Subtropical; average temperature in Jerusalem ranges from 5-13°C (41-55°F) in January to 18-31°C (64-88°F) in August
Main primary products Livestock, citrus fruits, grapes, wheat, sugar beet, cotton, olives, figs, vegetables; potash, crude oil, phosphates, bromine, natural gas
Major industries Agriculture, mining, food processing, textiles, clothing, leather goods, transport equipment, aircraft, chemicals, metal products, machinery, diamond cutting, fertilisers, cement
Main exports Finished diamonds, textiles, fruit, vegetables, chemicals, machinery, fertilisers
Annual income per head (US$) 8700
Population growth (per thous/yr) 16
Life expectancy (yrs) Male 72 **Female** 76

Children of Israel

The first Jews to reach Canaan (present-day Israel) were wandering migrants who, under the leadership of Abraham, moved there from northern Mesopotamia. They later settled in Egypt, where they were victims of persecution until the 13th century BC when another leader, Moses, was called upon by God to lead them out of bondage.

Their long and arduous journey back to Canaan took the Hebrews 40 years. But, throughout their trials, they were fortified by their religious faith. They were unique in their belief in one God, Jehovah, who would lead his chosen people to their 'Promised Land'. The basic principles of their faith were laid down in the Ten Commandments which, according to the Bible, were given to Moses by God on Mount Sinai.

After their return to Canaan, the Hebrews preserved their ancient tribal structure until they were united c. 1020 BC by a warrior-king Saul, to meet the challenge of the Philistines, a group of the marauding 'Sea Peoples' who had settled on the coastal plain of Palestine. Saul defeated the Philistines in several battles, and his successor, David, went on to complete his work, establishing a united Hebrew kingdom with its capital at Jerusalem c. 1000BC.

The rule of David's son, Solomon, saw Jewish power reach its height. But after Solomon's death c. 930 BC, the kingdom divided into two states, Israel and Judah, the latter ruled by the House of David, with its capital at Jerusalem. The two kingdoms warred and their disputes opened the way to foreign invasion.

Conquest and dispersion

Israel was the first of the two Jewish states to fall to an outside power when it was conquered by Assyria in 722 BC. After Assyria's fall, Judah was conquered by Babylon and the temple was destroyed. The 'Babylonian captivity' lasted for 50 years. When the Persians under Cyrus the Great captured Babylon in 539 BC, the Jews were allowed to return to their homeland and rebuild the Temple in Jersualem; but they did not regain full independence.

Persia was conquered by Alexander the Great in 331 BC, and after his death Greek dynasties battled for the division of his conquests. The Ptolemies controlled Israel until 198 BC, when they were driven out by the Seleucid ruler, Antiochus III. A Jewish revolt in 167 BC, led by Judas Maccabeus, ousted the Greeks. The Maccabean (Hasmonean) dynasty held power for 77 years before it was overthrown by the Romans.

Rome ruled Israel through a series of puppet kings. Under one of these kings, Herod Antipas, Jesus Christ embarked on his mission. The Jews could never reconcile themselves to Roman rule and in AD 66 revolt broke out, fomented by a group called the Zealots. Rome's reaction was harsh and brutal. Jerusalem fell to the Roman legions in AD 70 and the city's temple was again destroyed. The remnants of the rebel forces held out at Massada until AD 73, when they took their own lives rather than fall into Roman hands.

The Jewish spirit was not yet crushed. The Jews rose again in AD 132. Rome's reaction was even more severe. Many Jews were forcibly deported and their lands laid waste. Thus began the great Diaspora of the Jews. Milions of them settled in what were to become Christian countries of Europe – in lands such as Russia, Poland, Germany, Spain and England.

In many places the Jews were resented, for most Christians held them responsible for the death of Christ. They were confined to ghettos and forbidden to own land or to practise a trade. Many of them could only earn a living by lending money, a practice which further alienated them from Christians who, in medieval times, were forbidden to do so. Pogroms (persecutions) were commonplace.

For nearly 1900 years Palestine, as the Romans had renamed Israel, was ruled and fought over by foreigners. Romans, Byzantines, Sasanid Persians, Arabs, Crusaders and Turks all controlled it at various times. The few Jews who remained there were a subject people.

Birth of Zionism

In the 19th century, the Zionist movement was founded by the Hungarian Jew Theodor Herzl to press for the restoration of Palestine to the Jews. This movement grew rapidly, and increasing numbers of European Jews began to emigrate to Palestine. Financial aid came from American Zionists, as well as from Jewish philanthropists in Britain, such as Sir Moses Montefiore and Baron Edmond de Rothschild.

Towards the end of the First Word War, Palestine, which since 1517 had been ruled by Turkey, was conquered by Britain. Anxious for Jewish support, the British foreign secretary, Arthur Balfour, pledged British support for the Zionists in making Palestine a national home for the Jewish people.

But this pledge contradicted one given to the Arabs, who thought that Palestine was to become an independent Arab state after the war. When the war ended, the British, in fact, continued to rule Palestine under a League of Nations mandate.

Increasing Jewish immigration under the pressure of Nazi persecution in the 1930s alarmed the Arabs, who began to attack Jewish areas. The British then proposed to divide the country between the two groups. The Jews were prepared to discuss this plan, but the Arabs demanded full independence.

Foundation of modern Israel

After the Second World War, Britain decided to admit only 2000 Jewish immigrants a month. This decision alienated world opinion, which remembered the 6 million Jews that the Nazis had slaughtered in concentration camps. In Palestine itself, groups of Palestinian Jews – notably the Irgun Zvai Leumi and the 'Stern Gang' – began a terrorist campaign against British troops.

In 1947 the UN proposed that Palestine should be divided into Jewish and Arab states, with Jerusalem as a neutral zone. This plan was rejected by the Arabs but accepted by the Jews who, on May 14 1948, proclaimed the independent State of Israel. Chaim Weizmann was its first president, and David Ben Gurion its first prime minister. On the same day, the new state was attacked by Egypt, Jordan, Syria, Iraq and Lebanon. Israel emerged victorious from months of bitter fighting, having increased its territory by 50 per cent; some 700,000 Arabs fled from the Israeli-held lands.

Years of conflict and crisis

In spite of their defeat in 1948, the Arabs declared that they would never recognise Israel's right to exist. In 1956, Israel was again confronted by a hostile Arab military alliance, whose professed aim was the destruction of Israel. Israeli troops struck at Egypt. At the same time an Anglo-French invasion force was sent to safeguard the Suez Canal, which Egypt had just nationalised. United Nations' pressure forced Israel to give up most of its conquests. But the Israelis secured access to the Red Sea through the port of Elat on the Gulf of Aqaba.

The Egyptian blockade of Elat again led to war in 1967. Israel struck at Egypt, Syria and Jordan on June 5; in six days, its forces, under General Moshe Dayan, had captured the Gaza Strip, the Sinai Peninsula and the Golan Heights.

In October 1973, the fourth Arab-Israeli war began. It lasted only 18 days, but resulting economic losses to Israel were heavy. Currency was devalued and taxes were raised. When Menachem Begin became prime minister in 1977, he announced further austerity measures, introducing a new currency, the historic shekel, in an effort to curb inflation, then running at more than 100 per cent. In November 1977 Egyptian president Anwar Sadat offered to come to Jersualem. Begin invited him to address the Israeli parliament and so was broken the 30-year deadlock in which Arab leaders had refused to meet Israeli officials. Begin returned the visit at the end of 1977. Formal peace negotiations between the two nations began the next month and 14 months later, in March 1979, they signed a peace treaty. In May 1979 Israeli troops began to withdraw from Sinai and the first Israeli ships passed through the Suez Canal.

The problem of 2 million Arab Palestinian refugees in the areas surrounding Israel remains. The Palestine Liberation Organisation (PLO), recognised by Arab countries, has made many terrorist attacks on Israel, and Israel has retaliated by bombing Palestinian refugee camps. PLO forces, led by Yasser Arafat, were driven out of Lebanon in 1982 by an Israeli invasion aided by right-wing Lebanese Christian militiamen, but remain active elsewhere. The operation, involving a lengthy stay in Lebanon and the massacre by right-wing Lebanese of more than 700 Palestinian refugees in Israeli-occupied Beirut, brought worldwide criticism and political controversy in Israel; so did the settlement of Jews on the West Bank. In 1985, the Israelis withdrew from Lebanon.

The nation faced internal difficulties in the 1980s. The parliamentary elections of 1984 were contested by 15 parties; neither major party won a majority. After seven weeks of negotiations, a compromise was reached under which Shimon Peres, leader of the Labour Party, would serve as prime minister for 25 months with Yitzhak Shamir, leader of the Likud, as his deputy. At the end of that time the roles would be reversed.

Israel's economic and military survival has largely been made possible by the massive help it has received from the USA, both at government level and from the powerful American Jewish community. Israel is virtually self-supporting in foodstuffs, and a major exporter of agricultural produce. Its Jaffa oranges are famous throughout Europe, and it exports many other fruits and vegetables.

Much of its agriculture is based on methods employed at the kibbutz *(collective settlement) or* moshav *(cooperative village). The kibbutzim, with their organised communal life, are designed as agricultural collectives, but are also geared, especially in border areas, for rapid defence in times of war.*

There are 270 kibbutzim, with a total population of more than 110,000, scattered around the country. They produce 40 per cent of the country's agricultural output, but now there is hardly one without a factory as well – making electronic or irrigation equipment, processed foods, farm machinery or furniture.

A 1951 law gave Israeli women equal status with men, in theory at least – and there are women in uniform. Men and women serve side by side in the Israeli defence forces; the men do three years' national service, single women two. Married women are exempt.

There are 140,000 Israelis in the armed forces. Nearly a quarter of the national budget is spent on defence, and this puts a heavy strain on the economy. There are constant, huge balance of payments deficits, which are made good by aid from the USA, and Israel's inflation rate reached a staggering 1000 per cent a year in 1984.

In January 1991, following the first air attacks on Iraq by the UN-backed coalition forces, Iraq launched a series of missile attacks on Israel. Despite this provocation, Israel was not drawn into the conflict. In the aftermath of the Gulf War, America launched a peace initiative in the Middle East.

Saudi Arabia

One man, Ibn Saud, the leader of the Saudi tribe, was largely responsible for the creation of Saudi Arabia. He fought a prolonged war from 1902 to 1925 to bring the scattered tribes of Arabia under his rule. But the importance of this land to the Muslim world goes back 1400 years. It was at Mecca in 570 that the prophet Muhammad was born; today there are about 840 million followers of Islam throughout the world.

The discovery in 1935 of vast oil fields under its barren deserts transformed the country's economy. Today Saudi Arabia, with about a quarter of the known oil reserves, is the world's third largest oil producer.

Foundation of Islam: c. AD 600

Though organised communities existed in the far south of Arabia as early as 1000 BC, the area's importance began with the rise to power of the prophet Muhammad (570-632). After converting the nomadic Bedouin tribes to Islam, he formed a Muslim confederacy, with Medina as its capital. By the mid-8th century an Islamic empire stretched from the borders of India to Spain. But this empire had insecure foundations. Rivalry among its rulers and the formation of many sects in Islam itself led to its decline. By the mid-13th century Arabia had split up into many small sheikdoms.

Founding of the Saudi Nation

Much of Arabia had come under Turkish rule by the 16th century. This lasted until 1902 when the leader of the Saudi tribe, Abdul Aziz ibn Saud, embarked on a prolonged struggle to free the peninsula from the Turks. After Turkey entered the First World War against Britain in 1914, the British gave arms and aid to the Arabs. Colonel T.E. Lawrence ('Lawrence of Arabia') helped the tribes in an audacious guerrilla campaign against the Turkish forces. After the war, Ibn Saud fought his rivals to unify Arabia under Saudi rule. In 1927 Britain recognised Arabia's independence, and in 1932 it became the kingdom of Saudi Arabia.

Oil discovered

The development of the huge oil fields discovered in 1935 changed Saudi Arabia into one of the world's richest nations. Under Ibn Saud and his successor, Saud, it remained a conservative power.

Saud was replaced by his brother, Faisal, in 1964. Faisal started to share the country's new-found wealth with its people, building schools and hospitals.

During the Arab-Israeli war of 1973, Saudi Arabia took the lead in embargoing oil shipments to nations supporting Israel. King Faisal was assassinated in March 1975 by Prince Faisal bin Musaed. King Faisal's brother, Khaled Ibn Abdul Aziz, succeeded him. On Khaled's death in June 1982, Fahd, yet another son of Abdul Aziz ibn Saud, became king. The country remains an absolute monarchy; the king is also prime minister and owns all the undistributed land in the country. There are no elections and no political parties. There are about 5000 princes in the royal family and many important government offices are in their hands. Enlightened help for the people has gone hand in hand with royal extravagance: possibly 10 per cent of the oil wealth has gone to the royal family.

King Fahd, however, has said that he intends to create a majlis-al-shura *(consultative assembly). At first its members will be appointed. Later, half of them will be elected through a system of provincial assemblies.*

With massive oil revenues accumulating in the 1970s and early 1980s, Saudi Arabia adopted a policy of active diplomacy in the Middle East. In 1981 it played a key role in forming the six-member Gulf Co-operation Council. Later that year King Fahd put forward a peace plan to resolve the Arab-Israeli conflict. The 'Fahd Plan' subsequently became the Arab

SAUDI ARABIA AT A GLANCE

Area 830,000 square miles
Population 11,520,000
Capital Riyadh
Government Absolute monarchy
Currency Rial = 20 quirsh = 100 hallalas
Language Arabic (official), English
Religion Muslim (85% Sunni, 15% Shi'ite)
Climate Hot and dry, mild in winter; temperature in Riyadh ranges from 8-21°C (46-70°F) in January to 26-42°C (79-108°F) in July
Main primary products Cattle, goats, sheep, poultry, alfalfa, dates, grapes, water melons, wheat, sorghum; crude oil and natural gas
Major industries Crude oil and natural gas production and refining, cement, chemicals, fertilisers, steel
Main exports Crude oil and refined products, natural gas
Annual income per head (US$) 13,400
Population growth (per thous/yr) 30
Life expectancy (yrs) Male 53 **Female** 56

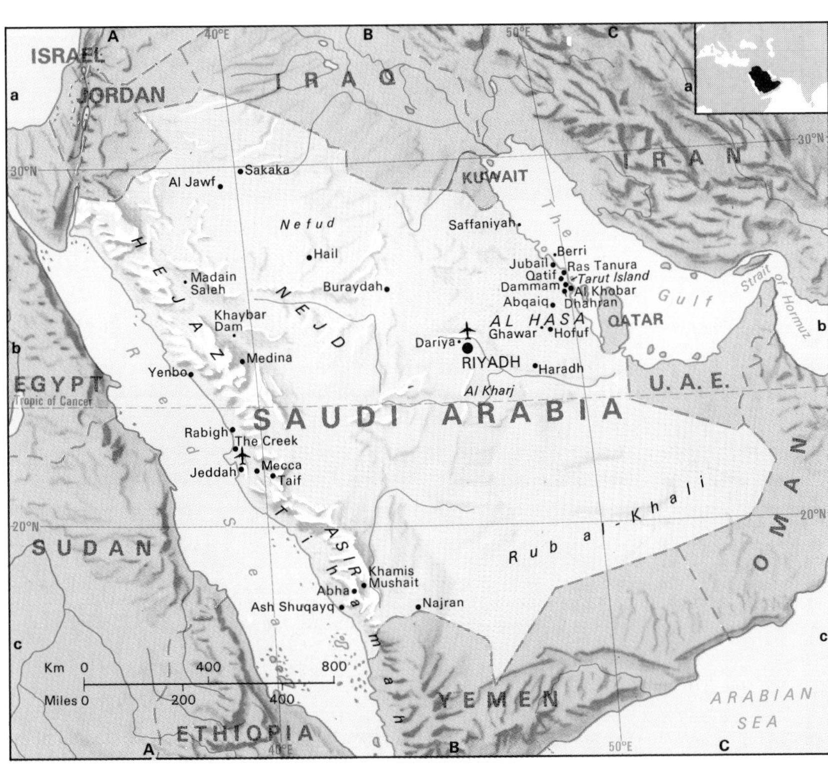

consensus proposal for resolving the conflict with Israel.

By 1985 Saudi Arabia was having to cope with the many problems brought on by the downturn in world oil markets. Production in the kingdom slid from a high of over 10 million barrels of oil a day in 1981 to less than 3 million in early 1985. Prices also sagged. As a result, the massive development budget was slashed and Saudi Arabia was forced to draw on its sizeable overseas investments. But expenditure on the military remained high, partly because of the continued threat posed by the Iran-Iraq war which had broken out in 1980.

The oil fields that are the source of nearly all the country's wealth lie in the eastern region, near and under the Gulf. Ghawar is the largest oil field in the world. It is 150 miles long and 22 miles wide and can produce 5 million barrels a day, more than twice the total production of Britain's North Sea oil fields. There are 46 other oil fields, although with falling demand only one-third are at present in production.

Development plans using the oil riches began with housing, schools and water supplies. At one stage three schools a day were being opened, and there are now 2 million students and seven universities. Education is free but illiteracy still remains high – about 60 per cent. Free land and interest-free loans are provided for housing, and there is now a surplus of apartments in Riyadh and Jeddah.

In the last ten years, 1750 factories have been built. Less than 1 per cent of the land is suitable for agriculture, but lavish subsidies increased grain production from 3000 tonnes to 1,300,000 tonnes a year. Large artificially watered market gardens sheltered beneath huge plastic sheets have been built, and at one time there was even a plan to tow Arctic icebergs into the Gulf to provide fresh water.

In August 1990, when Iraq invaded Kuwait, Saudi Arabia invited the UN-backed coalition troops to base themselves on its territory. In January 1991, Operation Desert Storm, the allied offensive to liberate Kuwait, was launched from Saudi Arabia.

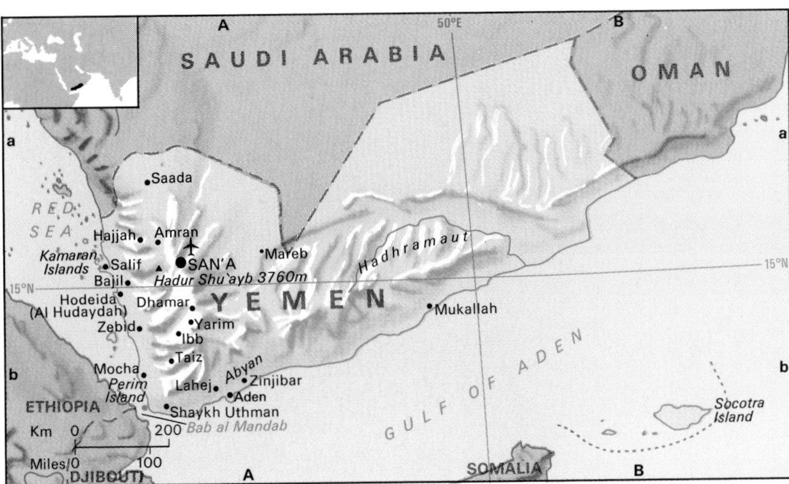

Yemen

In ancient times, Yemen was an important link in the trade route from the Mediterranean to the East. In 885 the Rassid dynasty started a period of rule which was to last in North Yemen until 1962.

For centuries the Muslim Imams (rulers) of Yemen kept their country in strict isolation from the outside world, despite Egyptian and then Turkish control of the coast. In 1839, however, the south came under British influence with the capture of Aden.

Only after the Second World War did the remainder of Yemen begin to pursue a more outward-looking policy. It became a partner in the United Arab Republic from 1958 to 1961.

Civil war: 1962-9

But change brought internal disturbance, and in 1962 the last Imam was overthrown by a republican revolution led by Col Abdullah al-Sallal and supported by Egyptian troops. The Yemen Arab Republic was established in September 1962. Republican control was soon established in the coastal Tihama area, while royalist forces held the highlands. Egypt, the Soviet Union, and Communist China supported the republicans in the ensuing civil war, while Saudi Arabia backed the royalists. The civil war ended in 1970 with agreement to include royalist leaders in future cabinets.

In 1974 the government was seized by the Military Command Council, which has since been in control. Soviet-supplied South Yemen troops invaded North Yemen in February 1979. In March the two nations agreed to a truce, and South Yemen withdrew its troops.

The government has taken care to remain friendly with both the Eastern and Western blocs. Saudi Arabia props up the country's economy with generous aid, arms are supplied by both America and Russia, and the Chinese and South Koreans are building roads. Ironically there is a serious shortage of skilled workers to develop the country – some 1.5 million Yemenis work elsewhere in the Arab world, but the money they send home is an important part of the economy.

South Yemen

For over a century Aden was an important military base from which the British wielded power in the Middle East and controlled the southern entrance to the Red Sea. Aden grew in size and importance after the Suez Canal opened in 1869, but the 20-odd sultanates and sheikdoms of the interior and coast remained undeveloped. Britain signed treaties with their rulers between 1882 and 1914, establishing them as protectorates under the governor of Aden. In 1963, despite local opposition, Aden was incorporated with the other states in the Federation of South Arabia. Britain promised this independence by 1968, but constitutional talks failed.

A guerrilla campaign against the British and the local rulers was mounted by the National Liberation Front (NLF) and the rival Front for the Liberation of South Yemen (FLOSY); the NLF emerged as the dominant group. When the British were forced to withdraw in 1967, the NLF declared independence and its Marxist wing took control. The sheiks fled or were deposed. Private owners were allowed 8 hectares (20 acres) of irrigated land, or 16 hectares (40 acres) without irrigation; the rest was redistributed. Banks, insurance and trading companies and the refinery were nationalised.

The Yemeni Socialist Party (including the NLF) was the only legal political party. The country was governed by a head of state who was also prime minister, and a supreme people's council of 111 members, elected by committees in each village.

The country was extremely backward until recent years, and remains poor by Arabian standards. It was almost entirely dependent on agriculture until a Texan company struck oil in 1984. The reserves have been estimated at a modest 300 million barrels, but production should soon be enough to supply Yemen's needs with some to spare.

Unification: 1989-90

In December 1989 an agreement was reached on a constitution for a unified state. On May 22, 1990, the Yemen Arab Republic (north) and the People's Democratic Republic of Yemen (south) were formally united as the Republic of Yemen. Multi-party elections are planned for the end of 1992.

YEMEN AT A GLANCE

Area 186,374 square miles

Population 12,000,000

Capital San'a

Government Republic

Currency Yemeni rial = 100 fils and Yemeni dinar = 1000 fils co-exist during transitional period following unification

Languages Arabic (official), English

Religion Muslim

Climate Hot and humid on the coast; cooler with summer rain in the hills. Temperatures at San'a average 14°C (57°F) in January; 22°C (71°F) in July

Main primary products Millet, sorghum, coffee, qat, cotton fruit, sesame, wheat, fish; crude oil

Major industries Agriculture, oil refining, handicrafts, cotton, textiles, leather goods, fishing, fish processing

Main exports Refined oil, processed fish, cotton, coffee, sugar, qat

Annual income per head (US$) 540

Population growth (per thous/yr) 28

Life expectancy (yrs) Male 44 **Female** 48

IRAQ AT A GLANCE
Area 167,925square miles
Population 16,000,000
Capital Baghdad
Government One-party socialist republic
Currency Dinar = 20 dirhams = 1000 fils
Languages Arabic; also Kurdish, Turkish and Assyrian
Religions Muslim (90%), Christian (10%)
Climate Hot summers, cool winters; average temperature in Baghdad ranges from 4-16°C (39-61°F) in January to 24-50°C (75-122°F) in July/August
Main primary products Sheep, dates, cereals, tomatoes, watermelons, cotton, cattle, goats, camels; crude oil, natural gas
Major industries Oil and gas production and refining, cement, chemicals, agriculture, food processing, brick making, textiles, leather
Main exports Crude oil and refined products, cotton, dates, cement, hides, wool
Annual income per head (US$) 2140
Population growth (per thous/yr) 33
Life expectancy (yrs) Male 55 **Female** 58

Iraq

This Arab country was the home of one of the world's earliest civilisations, that of Sumer. Mesopotamia, between the Tigris and Euphrates rivers, later saw the rise of Assyria and Babylon. Centuries after, the land fell under Arab rule and rose to greatness when Baghdad became the centre of Islamic civilisation.

The history of modern Iraq has been dominated by two factors – the wealth of its oilfields and the turbulence of its politics. The country's oil and its key strategic position in the Middle East have made it a source of rivalry between the West and the former USSR.

Dawn of history: 6000-1170 BC

Sumer, the southern part of ancient Mesopotamia, was a cradle of human civilisation. By c. 5000 BC, small communities in Sumer had adopted a settled way of life, based on agriculture. From them evolved city-states, such as Ur, Kish, Lagash and Uruk. By 3500 BC each of these had developed its own organised religion and government. Sumer was conquered c. 2300 BC by the Semitic people of Akkad, who occupied the north of Mesopotamia. Their king, Sargon, created an empire over the whole of Mesopotamia. After his death the empire broke up, but in 1792 BC, with the emergence of Hammurabi, King of Babylon, Mesopotamia was again united.

New Powers: 1170 BC-AD 638

Around 1170 BC, Babylon and other city-states of Mesopotamia became provinces of the Assyrian Empire, whose lands lay on the Upper Tigris River. Assyrian power reached its height under Assurbanipal (669-627 BC). But increasing inroads made by Egyptians, Medes and Babylonians brought this empire down. In 612 BC, Nebuchadnezzar, the Babylonian king, established the New Babylonian or Chaldean Empire – famed for its luxury and splendour. This, in turn, fell to Cyrus the Great, the Persian king; then to the Greeks under Alexander the Great, and finally to the Parthians, who turned the land into a battleground in their long conflict with the Romans.

Arab and Turkish rule

The area fell to the Arabs in AD 638 and Iraq became a Muslim country. Baghdad succeeded Damascus as capital of the Islamic empire in 762. This brilliant centre of art and learning was sacked by the Mongols in 1258 and again in 1401. Finally, in 1534, the country was conquered by Ottoman Turks and stayed under them for almost 400 years.

Iraqi nationalism: 1914-45

After the outbreak of the First World War, Britain invaded Turkish possessions in the Middle East, and occupied southern Iraq by 1915. The following year, a British attempt to take Baghdad failed but the city eventually fell in 1917.

British troops put down a nationalist rising in 1920, and the League of Nations made Iraq a mandated territory under the rule of Britain. An Arab prince, Faisal, was placed on the throne. Oil was discovered in Iraq in 1927. After the country was given independence in 1932, it maintained close links with Britain – a policy resented by many Iraqi nationalists. In the Second World War, the nationalist leader Rashid Ali al Gailani seized power. Britain intervened to overthrow him, because of his close ties with Germany and Italy.

Political turmoil

Iraq joined the Arab League in 1945 and took part in the unsuccessful military campaign against Israel in 1948. Under its pro-Western premier, Nuri es-Said, Iraq, though still opposed to Israel, led traditionalist Arab states in their opposition to the socialist policies of Nasser's Egypt from 1954 onwards. Iraq severed diplomatic relations with the USSR, and joined with Britain, Turkey, Iran and Pakistan in the Baghdad Pact defence treaty in 1955.

After Egypt and Syria had formed the United Arab Republic in 1958, Iraq and Jordan formed their own Arab union. But later that year, General Abdul Karim Kassem led a military coup in Baghdad. The king, Faisal II, and Nuri es-Said were killed, and Kassem proclaimed a republic. Iraq withdrew from the Baghdad Pact and re-established relations with the USSR.

But, at the same time, Kassem followed a strictly neutral foreign policy, putting down a pro-Communist rising in 1959. In his diplomacy he caused tension by challenging Egypt for Arab leadership. To add to his difficulties, war broke out with the Kurds, a non-Arab minority settled in north-eastern Iraq. The pro-Egyptian Abdul Salam Arif overthrew Kassem and had him executed in 1963. Arif also ousted the Baathists, the socialist party which had brought him to power.

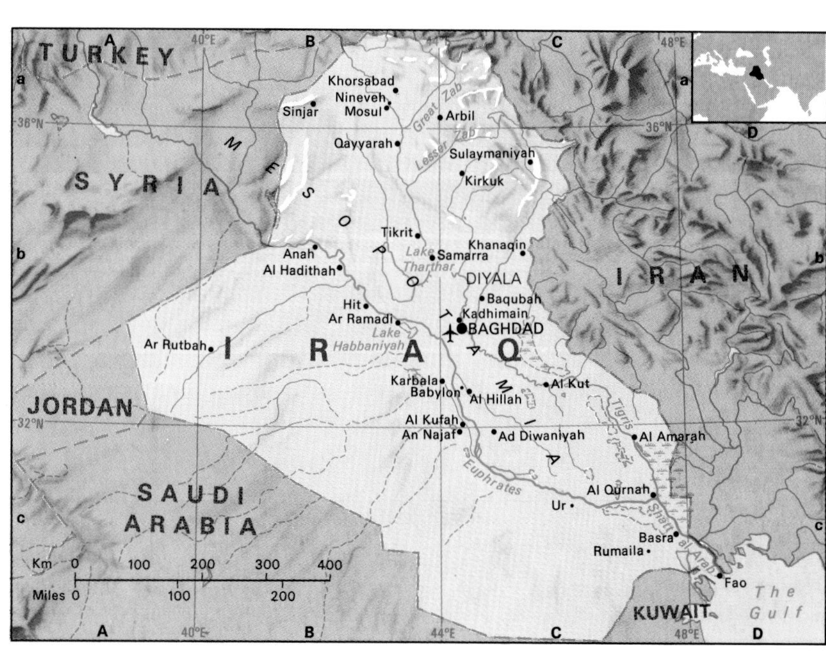

Arif was killed in a plane crash in 1966 and was succeeded by his brother, Abdul Rahman Arif. He in turn was ousted in 1968. Iraq's new government, under President Ahmed Hassan al-Bakr, was dominated by the Ba'athist Party, and dedicated to Arab unity and the destruction of Israel. In 1970 the Kurds were recognised as a separate nationality and given a degree of self-rule. But the Kurd rebellion continued, with military support from Iran. The revolt collapsed in March 1975 after Iran withdrew aid.

In the mid-1970s, like other oil-producing countries, Iraq profited from the great oil boom. The Kirkuk and Mosul oil fields of the north and that of Basra in the south were augmented by a new field found near Baghdad in 1975. By 1979 the country was producing 3 million barrels of oil a day. Prosperity descended on the land: cars, consumer goods, major development programmes providing new schools, hospitals, roads and factories. A free health service was established and unemployment virtually abolished by creating unproductive jobs.

That year Saddam Hussein, long regarded as the strong arm of his government, became president. Under him is a revolutionary council of nine members. A national assembly of 250 members is elected every four years, though the choice of candidates is limited. The only legal party is the National Progressive Front, composed of Ba'ath and Kurdish parties.

In 1980 Hussein launched a war against Iran which, having got rid of the Shah, was in the throes of Ayatollah Khomeini's revolutionary changes. It was the culmination of years of feuding over their shared river border along the Shatt al Arab. Khomeini's young armies resisted fanatically, and the war dragged on. Development programmes slowed down, and oil production fell to only 1 million barrels a day.

One of the disputes that divides the Arab world is about the importance of Ali. The Sunni, who comprise about 85 per cent of all Muslims, regard Ali as the fourth successor to Muhammad; the Shi'ites say he should rank first. Khomeini's Iran is Shi'ite, and fanatical; it condemns Iraq's President Hussein, a Sunni, as an unbeliever – and, to compound his sins, someone who expelled Khomeini when he was in exile in Iraq in 1978.

Iran constantly urges Iraq's milder Shi'ite majority to rise up against Hussein; so far they have shown little inclination to do so. Paradoxically, Iran has frequently shelled Basra, the main Shi'ite city.

In the early 1980s Iraq faced the problem of rapid change from a traditional, rural society to a modern, sophisticated, town-dwelling one. The urban population had quadrupled in the previous 25 years and accounted for more than 60 per cent of the population. Most of them are in the capital, Baghdad, which has a population of more than 3 million and most of the country's industry. The manufactures include carpets, leather goods, textiles, cement, tobacco products and arak. Basra, with a population of under half a million, is Iraq's only port. It has many oil refineries and normally exports petroleum products, wool, grain and dates.

Israeli jets destroyed a nuclear reactor near Baghdad in June 1981, claiming Iraq planned to use the reactor to produce atomic bombs.

When Iraq threatened in 1983 to use French Exocet missiles to destroy Iranian oil facilites, Iran warned it would retaliate by cutting off all shipping in the Persian Gulf. To protect its oil deliveries from Iranian attack, Iraq contracted in 1984 to build two pipelines. One will run through Jordan to the Gulf of Aqaba and the other through Saudi Arabia to the Red Sea port of Yanbu.

In August 1988 the United Nations arranged a ceasefire in the eight-year-old war between Iran and Iraq. UN sponsored peace talks continued the following year, and Iraq began to withdraw its troops from Iranian territory in August 1990.

On 2 August 1990, Iraqi troops invaded Kuwait. Within a week Saddam Hussein had declared the annexation of Kuwait. The UN Security Council voted to impose total economic sanctions on Iraq until it withdrew its forces from Kuwait. A coalition military force was sent to Saudi Arabia. At the end of November the Security Council authorised the use of force against Iraq if Iraqi troops were not withdrawn by 15 January 1991. Within 24 hours of the deadline passing, coalition forces launched air attacks on Iraq. The air bombardment continued for over a month. The land offensive was launched at the end of February, and Kuwait was liberated within days.

AFGHANISTAN AT A GLANCE
Area 251,772 square miles
Population 15,040,000
Capital Kabul
Government One-party republic
Currency Afghani = 100 puls
Languages Pushtu, Dari (Persian)
Religion Muslim
Climate Continental; average temperature in Kabul ranges from -8 to 2°C (18-35°F) in January to 16-33°C (61-91°F) in July
Main primary products Sheep, goats, fruit, wheat, cotton, nuts, vegetables; natural gas, iron, copper
Major industries Agriculture, fur and leather products, carpets, textiles, cement, glassware, bicycles, food processing
Main exports Fruit, nuts, natural gas, carpets, lambskins, cotton
Annual income per head (US$) 160
Population growth (per thous/yr) 17
Life expectancy (yrs) Male 36 **Female** 39

Afghanistan

The mountainous, land-locked country of Afghanistan did not develop a national identity until the 18th century. Before that time, its lands served as little more than a crossroads for conquerors and empire builders. They were part of the Persian Empire until c. 500 BC, and then eventually became part of Alexander the Great's vast conquests. After his death the country was ruled by other foreign overlords such as the Persians and Mughals until 1747.

Modern Afghanistan dates from the middle of the 18th century when Ahmad Shah, a tribal leader, established a united state covering most of present-day Afghanistan. For most of the 19th century the country was subjected to big-power pressures from Tsarist Russia in the north and the British in India to the east. Suspicions that its rulers were favouring the Russians led to the first two Afghan Wars with Britain (1838-42 and 1878-9). British forces were defeated both times, but returned in 1880 to enforce a treaty that gave them control of the Khyber Pass. By playing Britain and Russia off against each other, Afghanistan managed to remain independent, though under British influence.

Wars and reforms

In 1881 a new ruler, Abdurrahman Shah, came to power with British financial backing. He carried out reforms, and brought the rebellious tribes under firm government control.

Abdurrahman's successor, Habibullah, aroused the hostility of his Muslim subjects by remaining neutral in the First World War, instead of fighting on the side of the Muslim Turks, and he was assassinated in 1919. The new ruler, Amanullah, attacked the Indian frontier in order to arouse Afghan patriotism, but was speedily defeated by the British. At home, his reforms made him so unpopular that in 1929 civil war broke out and he was forced to flee the country.

Afghanistan was neutral in both World Wars, but relations with Pakistan have been strained since the partition of India and Pakistan's independence; the Afghans wanted the Pathans of the North-West Frontier to be given the chance to join Afghanistan.

Zahir Shah came to the throne in 1933. During the 1960s he introduced reforms to give the people of Afghanistan more voice in government, and settled a long standing dispute with Pakistan. But internal discontent grew, and in mid-1973 a move to overthrow the king plunged the country into crisis.

In 1973 King Muhammad Zahir was overthrown in a coup, and the monarchy ended after nearly 50 years. Afghanistan was declared a republic. Five years later President Muhammed Daoud was murdered in a second coup, which led to a Marxist government under Muhammad Taraki. In September 1979, Taraki was ousted in another coup and replaced by Hafizullah Amin. But, bitterly opposed by the people of the countryside, the government found it could maintain itself only by calling on the Soviet Union for help. The Soviet Union was happy to respond, realising an ambition to control their own 'back door' that goes back to Tsarist days. In December 1979 they invaded the country, deposed Amin and installed Babrak Karmal in his place. He was replaced as leader of the Afghan Communist Party by Major-General Najibullah in May 1986.

The rivalry between clans and their readiness to engage in fights or blood feuds now found a new outlet. The country was split between Marxist supporters, backed by the Soviet army, and resistance fighters providing fierce if uncoordinated opposition. Sometimes they fought among themselves. The 115,000 Russian troops, hampered by mountainous terrain and poor roads, found they were facing a brutal and bitter war against tribesmen renowned for their guerrilla tactics, who took to the hills to harass and strike.

The Russians relied mainly on bombing and ground sweeps, only to find that the guerrillas faded away when large numbers of soldiers appeared. They intensified the bombing to include crop-growing areas as well as villages: fields, stocks and herds were blitzed so that sowing times were missed and in some areas there was serious danger of famine. There were reports of atrocities on both sides.

But the war was costing the Russians the equivalent of US$1500 million a year. When President Gorbachev came to power in the Soviet Union in 1985 he realised that the fragile economy could ill afford this occupation. A withdrawal was agreed under the Geneva accords signed in April 1988 and by February the following year all 115,000 Soviet troops had left Afghanistan.

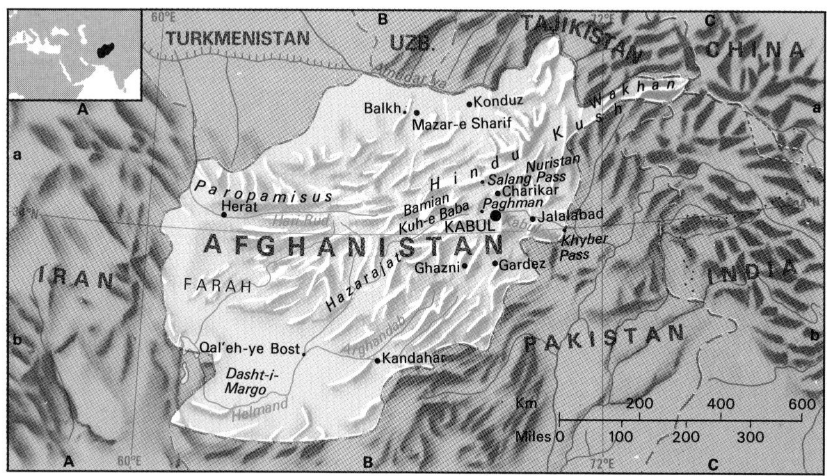

Picture Credits

p.9 C. Lénars; p.10 C. Kutschera; p.11 left F. Kohler; right C. Kutschera; p.12 left Jaffre-Durou; right R. McLeod; p.13 Gabanou-Diaf; p.14 top Michaud-Rapho; bottom C. Kutschera; p.15 C. Kutschera; p.16 J. Jaffre; p.17 Fishman-Contact-Cosmos; p.18 Boulat-Cosmos; p.19 R. McLeod; p.20 top R. McLeod; bottom A. Boucaud; p.21 Souse-Diaf; p.22 R. McLeod; p.23 top Michaud-Rapho; bottom Dupuis-Fotogram p.24 Reichel-Top; p.25 Michaud-Rapho; p.26 top Michaud-Rapho; bottom Thomas-Explorer; p.27 S. Held; p.28 Michaud-Rapho; p.29 S. Held; p.30 Michaud-Rapho; p.31 Michaud-Rapho; p.32 top C. Kutschera; bottom Gabanou-Diaf; p.33 S. Held; p.34 Fagot-Pix; p.35 Boulat-Cosmos; p.36 Michaud-Rapho; p.37 top Putelat-Top; bottom C. Kutschera; p.38 Michaud-Rapho; p.39 Putelat-Top; p.40 Michaud-Rapho; p.41 Oculi-Pix; p.42 Garcin-Diaf; p.43 top Fagot-Pix; bottom Garcin-Diaf; p.44 top Michaud-Rapho; bottom Michaud-Rapho; p.45 Gabanou-Diaf; p.46 top C. Kutschera; bottom C. Kutschera; p.47 C. Kutschera; p.48 Michaud-Rapho; p.49 S. Held; p.50 C. Lénars; p.51 left A. Hutchison Lby; right C. Kutschera; p.52 C. Kutschera; p.53 C. Lénars; p.54 top Goldman-Rapho; bottom C. Kutschera; p.55 Revault-Pix; p.56 C. Lénars; p.57 right Reininger-Contact-Cosmos; p.58 de Foy-Explorer; p.59 top Reininger-Contact-Cosmos; bottom Gerster-Rapho; p.60 Frilet; p.61 Harbutt-Cosmos; p.62 Bernager-Explorer; p.63 J.-P. Durand; p.64 top M. Riboud; bottom Harbutt-Cosmos; p.65 Reininger-Contact-Cosmos; p.66 Rousseau-Leda; p.67 Dorval-Explorer; p.68 Thomas-Explorer; p.69 Monty-Rapho; p.70 top P. & M. Maréchaux; bottom P. & M. Maréchaux; p.71 Gérard-Explorer; p.72 top P. & M. Maréchaux; bottom Gérard-Explorer; p.73 Constable-A. Hutchison Lby; p.74 C. Kutschera; p.75 left P. & M. Maréchaux; right P. & M. Maréchaux; p.76 C. Kutschera; p.77 Azzi-Woodfin Camp-Cosmos; p.78 top P. & M. Maréchaux; bottom P. & M. Maréchaux; p.79 C. Lénars; p.80 Azzi-Woodfin Camp-Cosmos; p.81 Gérard-Explorer; p.82 Gérard-Explorer; p.83 left P. & M. Maréchaux; right C. Lénars; p.84 Gérard-Explorer; p.85 Azzi-Woodfin Camp-Cosmos; p.86 top C. Lénars; bottom M. Riboud; p.87 M. Riboud; p.88 P. & M. Maréchaux; p.89 M. Maréchaux; p.90 top P. Maréchaux; bottom P. Maréchaux; p.91 Garcin-Diaf; p.92 C. Kutschera; p.93 Richer-Hoa-Qui; p.94 M. Maréchaux; p.95 left C. Kutschera; right Mazin-Top; p.96 P. Maréchaux; p.97 C. Lénars; p.98 left S. Held; right S. Held; p.99 S. Held; p.100 C. Kutschera; p.101 left C. Lénars; right Mazin-Top; p.102 Richer-Hoa-Qui; p.102/3 P. Frilet; p.103 P. Frilet; p.104 top P. Maréchaux; bottom P. Maréchaux; p.105 M. Maréchaux; p.106 C. Lénars; p.107 P. Maréchaux; p.108 Mazin-Top; p.109 Guenet-Lacontre-Gamma; p.110 top Gerster-Rapho; bottom C. Kutschera; p.111 C. Kutschera; p.112 Vuillomenet-Rapho; p.113 Gerster Rapho; p.114 left C. Kutschera; right C. Kutschera; p.115 C. Kutschera; p.116 Vuillomenet-Rapho; p.117 left Perno-Explorer; right C. Kutschera; p.118 C. Lénars; p.119 C. Kutschera; p.120 C. Kutschera; p.121 top C. Kutschera; bottom C. Kutschera; p.122 J. Le Moine; p.123 top C.Lénars; bottom Vuillomenet-Rapho; p.124 top C. Kutschera; bottom Vuillomenet-Rapho; p.125 C. Kutschera; p.126 Vuillomenet-Rapho; p.127 C. Kutschera; p. 128 C. Kutschera; p.129 Michaud-Rapho; p.130 top Schoenahl-Diaf; bottom Weisbecker-Explorer; p.131 Weisbecker-Explorer; p.132 M.F. de Labrouhe; p.133 Michaud-Rapho; p.134 Michaud-Rapho; p.135 left Michaud-Rapho; right Michaud-Rapho; p.136 Michaud-Rapho; p.137 Michaud-Rapho; p.138 Galichet-Diaf; p.139 top Michaud-Rapho; bottom Michaud-Rapho; p.140 Michaud-Rapho; p.141 Michaud-Rapho; p.142 top Michaud-Rapho; bottom Michaud-Rapho; p. 143 Michaud-Rapho; p.144 Michaud-Rapho; p.144/5 Michaud-Rapho; p.145 Michaud-Rapho; p. 146 Michaud-Rapho; p.146/7 Michaud-Rapho; p.147 Michaud-Rapho; p.148 Michaud-Rapho

Cover pictures:
Top: Peter Knapp-The Image Bank
Bottom: Lisl Dennis-The Image Bank